Filet Lace
Stitches and Patterns

Filet Lace
Stitches and Patterns

MARGARET MORGAN

SALLYMILNER
PUBLISHING

First published in 2006 by
Sally Milner Publishing Pty Ltd
PO Box 2104
Bowral NSW 2576
AUSTRALIA

© Margaret Morgan 2006

Design: Anna Warren, Warren Ventures
Editing: Anne Savage
Photography: Tim Connolly

Printed in China

National Library of Australia Cataloguing-in-Publication data:

Morgan, Margaret.
    Filet lace.

    Bibliography.
    ISBN 9781863513654.

    ISBN 1 86351 365 5.

    1. Needlepoint lace - History. 2. Needlepoint lace -
    Patterns. 3. Lace and lace making. I. Title. (Series :
    Milner craft series).

    746.224

10 9 8 7 6 5 4 3 2 1

Acknowledgments

This book would not have been written without the support of a number of people. Firstly I would like to acknowledge my debt to two people, both of whom died some years ago. One is Miss Pauline Knight, the author of two books on filet lace, with whom I corresponded for a number of years, and whom I met twice in England before she died aged 101 years. The other is Mrs Jean Lange, who was the only person I knew in South Australia who did filet lace. Jean constantly encouraged me, and I still find inspiration in her example. Next, I would like to thank the members of the Australian Lace Guild and the Embroiderers' Guild of South Australia. Both Guilds have given me the opportunity to share my knowledge of filet lace by holding workshops, and their members have supported these workshops by their attendance. The lessons in this book are based on the classes I have given for these two Guilds. Thirdly, my thanks go to my friend Anne McGowan, whose enthusiasm spurs me on to achieve more than I would on my own, and who kindly proofread the manuscript for me. And finally, I would like to thank my husband, John, who has always supported me in every project I have undertaken, with love, patience, and active assistance.

Contents

Introduction

HISTORY

Filet lace is one of the oldest forms of lacemaking, predating bobbin lace and most forms of needlelace. In brief, it can be described as embroidery on a net with a square mesh (as opposed to the hexagonal mesh of tulle), and until the invention of machines capable of reproducing the net, this net was of necessity hand-made. Presumably the craft had its origins in ancient times, when plain netting, as used for fishing nets, was developed and refined for making hair nets and dresses, which were then further embellished with embroidery of gold and silken threads. Filet lace has persisted through the centuries, in the Middle Ages being much used for ecclesiastical purposes. For example, an Exeter Cathedral inventory of 1327 lists three pieces of darned netting for use at the altar. In the Renaissance period filet lace was popular, as is shown by its inclusion in the first printed lace pattern books. One of these books was Federico Vinciolo's *Singuliers et nouveaux pourtraicts of 1587*, of which a facsimile edition is now available, entitled *Renaissance Patterns for Lace, Embroidery and Needlepoint*. Two famous sixteenth century women, Catherine de Medici and Mary Queen of Scots, were both enthusiastic workers of filet lace.[1]

Over the years filet lace has been known by many names. 'Lacis' is the term under which it is generally classified by museums and history books. However, there is a long list of other names which have been used to refer to it, including *opus araneum, opus filatorium, ouvrages*

---

1. For a picture of a piece of filet lace said to have been worked by Mary, see Margaret Swain's *The Needlework of Mary Queen of Scots*, page 93

maschés, *punto ricamato a maglia*, Cluny guipure lace, *filet brodé à reprises* and *Modàno*.

Some of these variations are due to different terms being used at different times (for example, *opus araneum* and *ouvrages maschés* were medieval terms), or to different terms being use in different countries (for example, *filet brodé* is a French term while *punto ricamato* is Italian). Sometimes the different terms indicate different styles of filet, such as 'filet Richelieu' and 'filet guipure'. However, this can be confusing, as different authors can use the same term in different ways. The *Anchor Manual of Needlework*, for example, uses the term 'Cluny filet' for designs worked solely in 'lace stitch' (presumably linen stitch), whereas Mrs Jackson writes of 'Cluny guipure lace' and says that it is distinguished 'by raised stitches, wheels, circles, and triangles'.[2]

Although there are many stitches used in filet, much old filet was worked using one stitch only, linen stitch (also known as *point de toile*). For this reason linen stitch is usually regarded as the basic stitch of filet lace. Some filet lace, however, is worked using linen stitch as the basis of the design, with an outlining thread (often a thicker thread) which outlines and connects the sections of linen stitch, and also adds decorative scrolls and tendrils. This style of filet is usually referred to as filet Richelieu and also has a long history. Pauline Knight, in her book *The Technique of Filet Lace*, includes a photograph of a piece of filet of this type which is dated to 1620 and another German piece dated to the sixteenth century.[3] Filet Richelieu was popular in the late nineteenth and early twentieth centuries, and DMC produced a publication entitled *Le Filet-Richielieu par Th. de Dillmont*.

Another style of filet, generally referred to as filet guipure, is characterised by a variety of stitches, including both filling stitches and raised stitches. It is most often seen on early twentieth century tablecloths and mats which were imported from China. These

---

2. Mrs F. Nevill Jackson, *Old Handmade Lace*, page 137.
3. Pauline Knight, *The Technique of Filet Lace*, pages 20 ff and page 40.

tablecloths and mats were worked on a knotted net of large mesh. This type of filet is once again appearing in shops, again imported. However, filet guipure is not a recent invention, as is shown by the fact that Vinciolo in his book included designs which appear to have elements of a guipure style.[4]

No doubt there are many other styles of filet, as it is a technique which appears to have a long history in many countries, and which therefore is bound to exhibit regional variations. One of these regional variations is the filet lace produced in Finland to decorate traditional bonnets. The net was a fine hand-knotted one which differed from most other filet nets in that a design of larger holes was incorporated into the net itself before being embroidered. The Finnish filet also has a different technique of darning the pattern into the net. With the advent of machine-made materials, the use of tulle gradually ousted hand-knotted net for these head-dresses, although in recent years in Finland there has been a revival of interest in the traditional technique.

One other type of filet is *buratto*. This name derives from the Latin word burra, meaning a shaggy garment, and *buratto* was a loosely woven square-meshed fabric which was used for filet embroidery in place of the knotted net. It could be argued that buratto is closer to modern-day filet than the old knotted filet, because most modern-day embroiderers use a woven base (machine-woven) for their filet in preference to the time-consuming process of knotting their own net. Buratto dates back to the sixteenth century, and was produced mainly in Italy.

Filet lace is a lace technique which has stood the test of time, as is shown by its long history. In the early years of the twentieth century it was extremely popular among needlewomen, and numerous pattern books for filet were published. Although interest in filet declined in the middle years of the last century, along with interest in many other needle arts, in the later years interest was rekindled, especially with the

---

4.   Federico Vinciolo, *Renaissance Patterns for Lace, Embroidery and Needlepoint,* pages 54, 56, 70, 73.

publication of Miss Pauline Knight's books on filet lace in 1980 and 1990. Unfortunately, these books are now out of print. With interest in filet once again growing, some of the old pattern books have been republished, but there is a need for a book to instruct beginners in the techniques of the lace. It is hoped that this book will go some way in doing this and assist in the resurgence of interest in such a beautiful and historic lace.

MATERIALS

Nets

There are a number of nets which can be used for filet lace. Some are made specifically for filet, and some are made as curtain material but can be used for filet because they consist of square (or nearly square) meshes. The most readily available nets are:

6 holes per inch polycotton net (available in white or ecru)

9 holes per inch polycotton net (white only)

14 holes per inch cotton net (white or cream)

There are also larger count cotton and synthetic nets available (5 hpi or even larger), which are knotted rather than woven nets. Finer count

Doll's house runner worked in darning stitch, actual size

woven nets can found by searching in curtain stores. These are usually synthetic nets. The doll's house runner pictured here is made on synthetic curtain net.

Threads

A variety of threads can be used for filet lace. Pearl cotton is a good thread for learning darning stitch and linen stitch, because it is a soft thread which does not twist or tangle too much while working. But it is interesting to experiment with a number of different threads, as you can achieve different effects and textures in this way. Sewing cottons and bobbin lace threads are very useful, especially for some of the fine filling stitches or when working on a smaller count net. Silk thread, with its beautiful sheen, can highlight parts of a design.

Needles

A blunt needle is best for filet lace. A tapestry needle can be used— choose a size which takes your thread comfortably. However, there is another needle which is ideal for filet lace. This needle is called a reweaving needle, and is a long needle with a little ball on the end. The length of the needle makes weaving long rows easier, and the little ball helps to keep your thread on the needle as you are weaving. These needles come in a number of different sizes, in lengths ranging from 2.5 to 9 cm (1 to 3.5 inches). These needles are not readily available and you are unlikely to find them in needlework shops. They can be purchased from specialist lace suppliers.

Frames

Traditionally, square or rectangular frames were used for filet lace. These were simple wire frames, and the net was sewn onto the frame before beginning to stitch the design. Embroidery hoops can be used for filet, but be sure to keep the net as straight as possible in the frame. If you use an embroidery hoop, remove your work from it when you finish stitching for the day (so that you do not get a hoop mark on your lace if it is left in the hoop for a long time), and make sure that when you cut out your material, you allow enough material to accommodate the frame: allow at least 5 cm (2 inches) on each side of your design, or more if you intend to frame the finished article.

NOTES ON THE DESIGNS

The small projects in the lessons in the first part of this book were all stitched on a 9 count (i.e. 9 holes per inch) net, and these pieces can be used for mounting in greeting cards or in coasters. However, they could also be stitched on a different count net. In the charts for these projects I have used the symbol # for linen stitch. In the *diagrams*, however, I have used a cross to mark the meshes which are to be filled with linen stitch. I have done this for the sake of clarity, so that the route of the thread can be drawn over the top of the crosses.

In the second part of the book many of the patterns can be stitched in either linen stitch or darning stitch. Where this is the case, I have used the symbol ■ on the chart, and you can choose for yourself whether you stitch these patterns in linen or darning stitch. Some of the charts in this part of the book are quite large and consequently are difficult to print on a single page in a large scale. It is suggested that you enlarge these charts on a photocopier before attempting to stitch them.

Lesson 1
Darning stitch and simple linen stitch

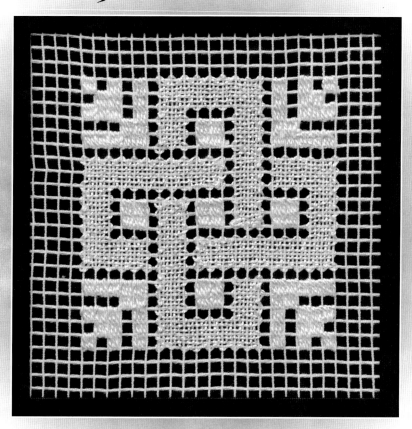

Worked on 9 count net, using DMC Pearl 8 for
darning stitch and Pearl 12 for linen stitch.
See graph and stitching instructions on
pages 21 to 24.

DARNING STITCH

Of the many stitches which can be used in filet lace,
darning stitch is probably the simplest. It is also a very
old stitch, as is shown by the fact that some designs in
Vinciolo's book clearly suggest its use. The French name
for darning stitch is *point de reprise*, and you will see this
term used in some old publications. As the name
implies, for darning stitch the embroidery thread is
darned over and under the threads of the net. The
patterns can be darned either horizontally or vertically,
or with a combination of both, which can give an
interesting play of light. Many designs can be worked
using this stitch alone, and lace of this type is often
referred to as lace net embroidery or net darning.

Following diagrams 1a–1c, and leaving a 10 cm
(4 inch) tail of thread, pass the needle over and under
the threads of the net. Turn and come back in the
opposite direction, making sure that you go under the
threads of the net that you went over in the first run.

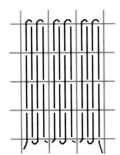

Diagram 1a
Darning stitch

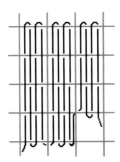

Diagram 1b
Darning stitch: one
way of decreasing

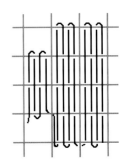

Diagram 1c
Darning stitch: one way
of increasing

Repeat this process until the squares are full (this varies with the size of the net and the thread used, but generally takes four to six runs). Hide the ends of the thread at the back of your work by darning under the completed stitches.

> **NOTE** In diagrams 1a–1c the starting point for the thread journey is at the bottom left-hand corner. This does not mean that the actual stitching must always start at the bottom left-hand corner. Left-handed embroiderers are at no disadvantage, as it is possible to work from left to right, right to left, top to bottom, or bottom to top.

LINEN STITCH

Linen stitch is the main stitch of filet lace, its name deriving from the fact that in appearance it is like a woven piece of linen. Many old examples of filet lace were worked entirely in linen stitch. Traditionally, linen stitch consists of two horizontal threads and two vertical threads per mesh of the net (diagram 2). Because old filet lace was mostly worked on a fine hand-knotted net, two horizontal and two vertical threads were sufficient to fill the holes of the net. If a net with a large mesh is used, however, it is necessary either to use a thick thread, or to increase the number of runs per row and have four horizontal and four vertical threads. In the early part of the twentieth century a large mesh net was often used, and so some instruction books and magazines produced at that time depict in their diagrams four threads per row. The instructions given below follow the traditional method and assume that there will be only two threads per row.

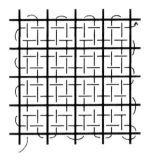

Diagram 2
Traditional linen stitch

Following diagram 2, and leaving a 10 cm (4 inch) tail of thread at the front of the work, pass the needle over and under the threads of the net. Turn and come back in the opposite direction, making sure that you go under the threads of the net that you went over in the first run. Proceed to the next row, but when changing rows make sure that you start at the very bottom of the row (i.e. in the hole immediately adjacent to the one where you have just finished—*do not* go diagonally from the mesh of the first row to the mesh of the next row). The edge of the design where you change from one row to another should look 'loopy' (see diagram 2, at bottom and right side of diagram).

Linen stitch has something of the elements of a puzzle, for theoretically in a correctly worked design the route of the thread should be one long continuous line and should end back where it started. When working in linen stitch it is necessary to leave some squares only half-worked at first, to be completed later. The reason for this is that the thread should travel unbroken along the entire length of each individual row of the design. An example of this appears in diagrams 3a and 3b, where 3a shows the correct method of working the design, and 3b an incorrect method.

Diagram 3a
Correct method (note 90°
turns in rows a and b)

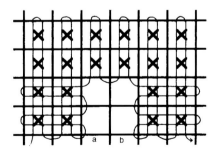

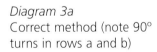

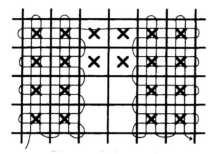

To complete the design in diagram 3a you use edge stitch to get back to the incomplete rows and then edge stitch along the top and down the left-hand side to get back to the start (see diagram 5).

Joining threads: join threads with a reef knot. It is a good idea to work a little way with the new thread before knotting the old and the new threads together. This makes it easier to position the knot at an inconspicuous spot at the back of the work.

EDGE STITCH

When working edge stitch you pass over and under the threads of the net as in darning and linen stitch, but as well as that you catch in the loops of the previously worked linen stitch (diagram 4). You must be sure to keep in a strict over and under sequence.

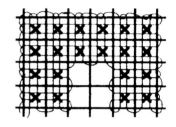

Diagram 3b
Incorrect method

Diagram 5
Completion of diagram 3a
using edge stitch

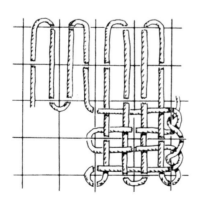

Diagram 4
Edge stitch

NOTE If the needle has just passed over a bar of net it will pass *under* the net to come up into the loop. If it has just passed under a bar it will pass *over* the net and down into the loop (over and up, under and down).

Besides getting you back to where you want to go, edge stitch gives a rounded appearance to all edges and corners.

TIPS TO CHECK THAT YOUR LINEN STITCH IS CORRECT

◆ overs/unders should match on either side of a bar of the net (the bar of the net counts as the opposite under/over)—see diagram 4.

◆ the loops at the bottom of a piece of linen stitch should go over, under, over, under, etc.—see diagram 4 at bottom of diagram.

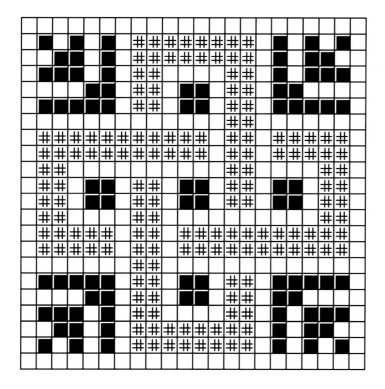

Section 1

■ darning stitch: DMC Pearl 8

linen stitch: DMC Pearl 12

Stitching instructions

Each square on the graph represents one mesh of the net. The graphed design shows the area to be filled with stitching, the rest is left blank.

As darning stitch is the easier stitch, it is probably best to work the darning stitch sections first. Make sure that you count carefully so that they are placed in the correct position, and that you leave the right number of meshes for working the linen stitch sections. Work with your net in an embroidery hoop.

Linen stitch

Work section 1, on the right-hand side of the design, following the diagram. When you have completed this section, work the other three sections, which are simply repeats of the first section. By turning your work 90° after finishing each section, you can work each section in exactly the same way, following the diagrams. However, there is no correct starting point. If you are confident that you understand the technique, you could start each section in a different spot, which is good practice. The end result should be the same. When starting each new section make sure that you count the meshes carefully so that it is in the correct position.

Diagrams 6a–6d are an enlargement of section 1 of the graph, showing the route of the thread for linen stitch.

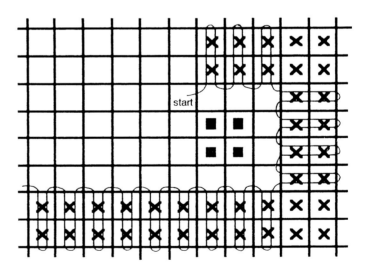

Diagram 6a Darn your threads over and under the net, following the route shown.

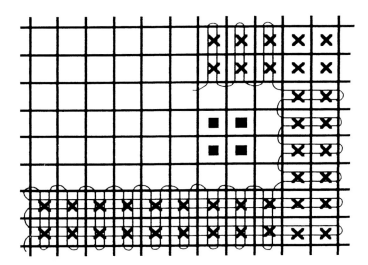

Diagram 6b Turn the corner and work the two rows as shown, weaving over and under both the threads of the net and the threads which you have previously laid down. Make sure that you go over 11 meshes in each row (i.e. 2 meshes past the threads you have laid down). When turning a corner be careful that you do not cut the corner by going diagonally from the end of one row to the beginning of the next. The thread must go into the corner mesh or your weaving will not work out properly (refer back to diagram 4 to see how to go around a corner).

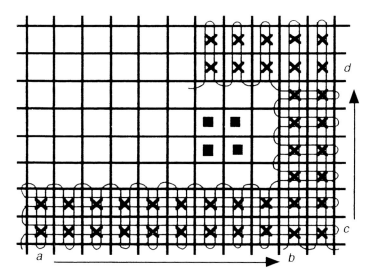

Diagram 6c Turn the corner and, starting at point **a**, work edge stitch all along the side (as indicated by the arrow) until you get to point **b**. At point **b**, weave two rows (making sure that you go over a total of 8 meshes) and then turn the corner. Beginning at **c**, edge stitch all along the side (as indicated by the arrow) until you get to point **d**.

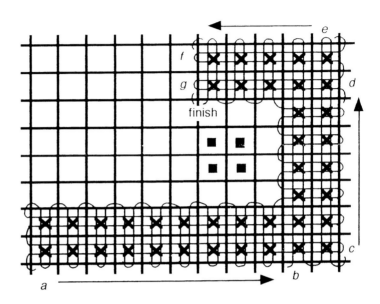

Diagram 6d Weave two rows, and then turn the corner. From point **e** edge stitch along the side. Turn the corner and work edge stitch at **f** and **g**. Turn the corner and at the back of the work knot the beginning and ending threads together. Hide the ends by weaving them in a short way along the edge of the work. Trim thread.

PRACTICE CHARTS

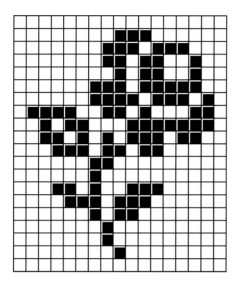

A simple pattern of a rose for practising darning stitch

■ darning stitch

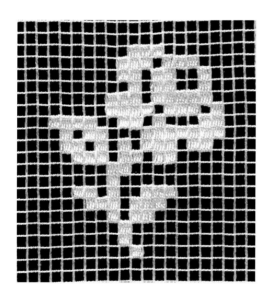

The rose worked on 9 count net, using DMC Pearl 8

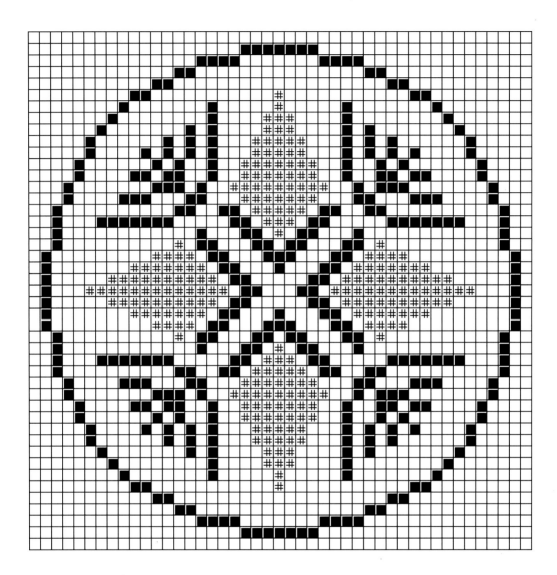

A simple pattern for practising darning stitch and linen stitch

■ darning stitch

\# linen stitch

Lesson 2
Linen stitch with holes, and loop stitch

Worked on 9 count net, using DMC Pearl 12 for
darning stitch and linen stitch and sewing cotton
for loop stitch.
See stitching instructions on page 34.

WORKING HOLES IN LINEN STITCH

Many filet lace designs incorporate holes within the
linen stitch, for the holes help make the embroidery
look 'lacy'. These holes should appear round, not square.
To achieve this a special rule is followed. Whenever the
thread enters a mesh of the net which is to be left as a
hole, you immediately make a 90° turn. If you are
travelling along the left side of a row you turn 90° left at
the hole; if you are travelling along the right side of a
row, then you turn 90° right. It will be obvious if you
turn the wrong way as your threads will cross when you
get back to the spot where you started working the hole,
and you will not have a nice round hole.

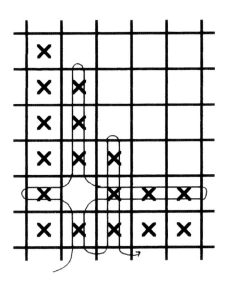

Diagram 7 Working a
hole in linen stitch

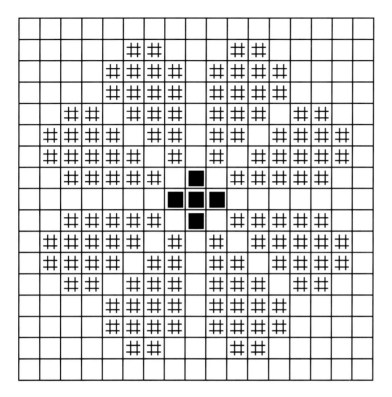

Practice pattern for working holes

■ darning stitch

linen stitch

It is advisable, until you are experienced, to mark the holes in some way on your graph to make them easy to notice (a red dot serves very well).

Stitch the centre of this flower in darning stitch and the petals in linen stitch. Each petal is identical and so can be stitched in the same way simply by rotating your work. There are three holes in each petal and to work these correctly you must follow the instructions for working holes in linen stitch; that is, every time you enter the mesh where the hole is to be, you turn 90°. In the diagram below the route of the thread is shown for one petal. The edge stitches are indicated by the thin lines. The pale grey grid lines represent the threads of the net.

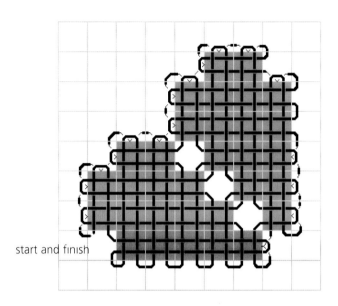

start and finish

Diagram 8
Route of thread for one petal

LOOP STITCH

Loop stitch is a useful filling or background stitch. It can be used to lighten a design and give the embroidery a very delicate look. To achieve this effect a finer thread than that used for linen stitch is necessary. Loop stitch is essentially a loose buttonhole stitch. You work the first half of each stitch right along to the end of the row, and then complete the stitches on the return journey (diagrams 9a and 9b). Subsequent rows are worked in the same way, except that, as well as looping over the bar of the net, you need to catch in the loop of the previous row (diagram 9c).

There are two methods of completing a section of loop stitch. One method (diagrams 9a–9d) is to leave the beginning of each row only partly worked at first. When you have worked the bottom row of loop stitch, you then complete the first column of stitches by working up from point d back to point a (see diagram 9e), where you knot the beginning and ending threads together.

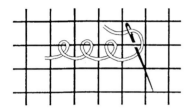

Diagram 9a
First half of loop stitch

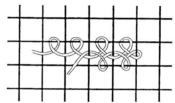

Diagram 9b
Return journey

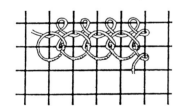

Diagram 9c
First half of next row (shaded)

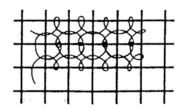

Diagram 9d
Return journey of next row, showing the circular effect of the stitch

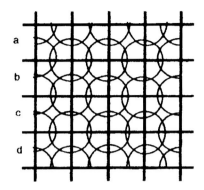

Diagram 9e Completed
section of loop stitch

Another method is shown in diagrams 10a–10d. Secure
your thread at the intersection of the net, whip down to
the middle of the bar, and commence the first row.
Complete the first row back to point a (diagram 9e).
Then whip down to point b and start the next row, and
so on. When you have finished the section of loop stitch,
secure the thread with a couple of half-hitch knots and
hide the end of the thread.

When you are filling an irregular shape with loop
stitch, the second method is usually preferable as it is
easier to control the tension and keep the work neat. Just
remember that when you complete each row you simply
whip to the spot where you want to start the next row. If
you are working with a fine thread the whipping will be
hardly noticeable.

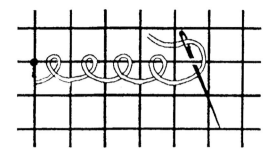

Diagram 10a
First half of loop stitch

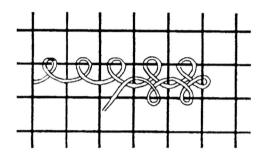

Diagram 10b
Return journey

Diagram 10c
First half of
next row (shaded)

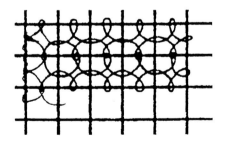

Diagram 10d
Return journey
of next row, showing
the circular effect of
the stitch

33

Stitching instructions

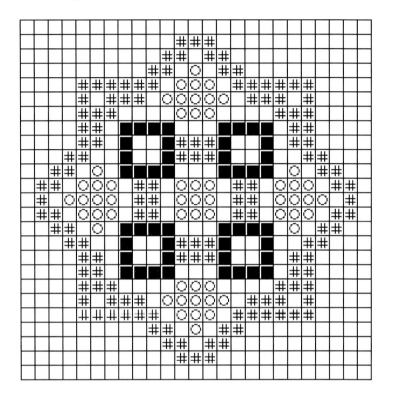

■ darning stitch

linen stitch

○ loop stitch

Work the linen stitch sections near the centre of the design first. Then work the outer section of linen stitch. Begin from the outside edge of the design, working towards the inside edge (i.e. the tail of thread at the beginning of your work will be on the outer edge of the design, not the inside edge). If you do this, the outside edge of the lace will be 'loopy', whereas the inside edge will be straighter (see the photograph of the worked lace at beginning of this lesson). It does not matter where you begin the linen stitch, but a convenient point would be immediately below the bottom hole on the left. Then you would begin this section of linen stitch as shown previously in diagram 7, working a hole.

Next work the loop stitch sections, starting with the square in the centre. Use a fine thread for the loop stitch and a thicker thread for linen and darning stitch.

Finally, work the darning stitch sections.

PRACTICE CHART

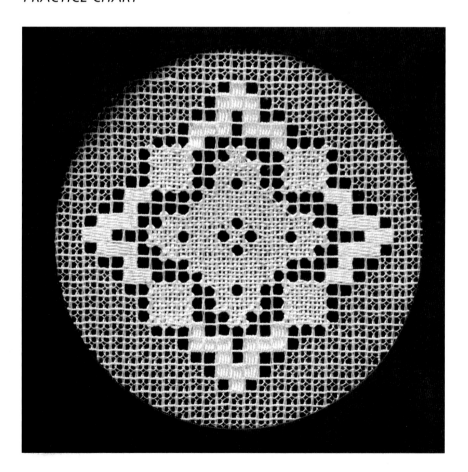

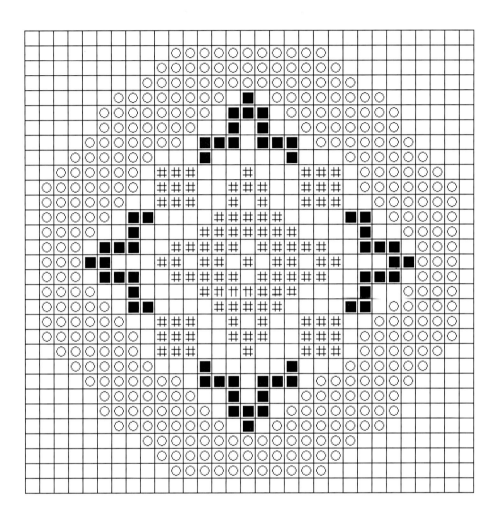

29 meshes high x 29 meshes wide

■ darning stitch

linen stitch

○ loop stitch

Lesson 3
Linen stitch with
holes forming a square

**Worked on 9 count net, using DMC Pearl 12 for
darning stitch and linen stitch.
See stitching instructions on page 41.**

HOLES: EXCEPTIONS TO THE RULE

Holes forming squares or rectangles

When holes are positioned in a design in such a way that
they form the corners of a square or a rectangle, it is
necessary to break the rule on holes as outlined in lesson
2, for otherwise parts of the design will not be able to be
worked. At one of the holes that form the corners of the
square, instead of making a 90° turn make a 360° turn
so that you can get into the centre of the square.
Continue working until you return to this hole, at which
point you edge-stitch into the loop and come out at the
other side of the hole (see diagram 11). Then continue as
normal.

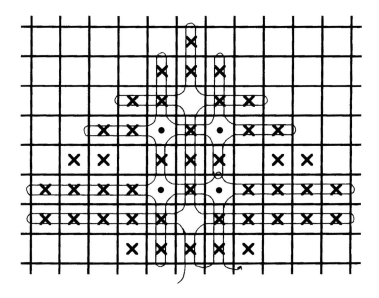

Diagram 11 Holes
forming a square
(indicated by the dots).
Note that a different
starting point could be
chosen.

Do not despair if you find, on completing a design, that you have forgotten to allow for holes forming a square or rectangle and that consequently there is a thread missing on the inside of the square or rectangle. This thread can always be added in separately afterwards.

BUTTONHOLE STITCH EDGING

If you are mounting your piece of lace in a frame of some sort, then you do not need to finish off the raw edges of the net as these will be hidden by the frame. If you wish to make a mat or doily, however, then you need to have an edge to your work. The traditional edging for filet lace is a buttonhole stitch edging.

Work two rows of whipping all around the edge of the mat (see diagram 12b). The thread you use for the whipping will depend on the count of the net you are using and also on the finished effect you want. You can use the same thread that you use for the buttonhole stitch (diagram 12a), but if you wish to reduce the bulk of the edging you can choose a finer thread, for example, sewing cotton.

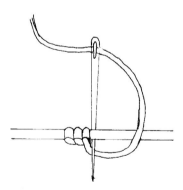

Diagram 12a
Buttonhole stitch

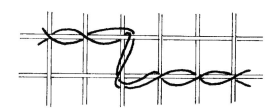

Diagram 12b
Whipping

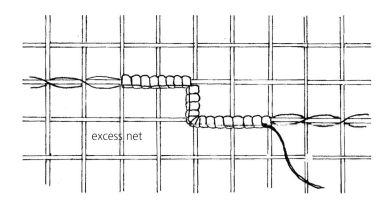

excess net

Diagram 12c
Buttonhole stitches

Next, work close buttonhole stitches over the top of the whipped thread (diagram 12c). Finally, carefully cut away the excess net close to the buttonhole stitches.

Stitching instructions

Work the linen stitch sections of the pattern first. Once you have completed the linen stitch, work the darning stitch. Work the darning stitch all in the same direction (i.e. either horizontally or vertically).

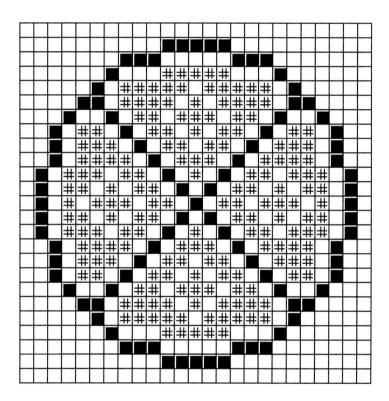

23 meshes high x 23 meshes wide

■   darning stitch

linen stitch

PRACTICE CHART

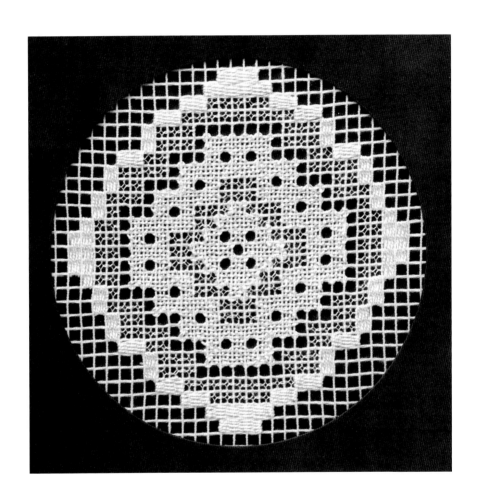

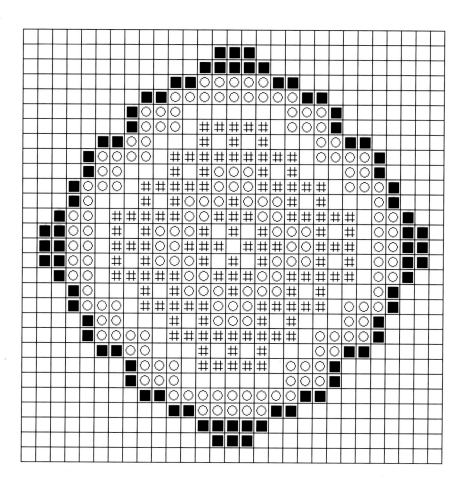

27 meshes wide x 27 meshes high

■ darning stitch

linen stitch

○ loop stitch

Lesson 4
Linen stitch with holes in parallel lines, and oblique loop stitch

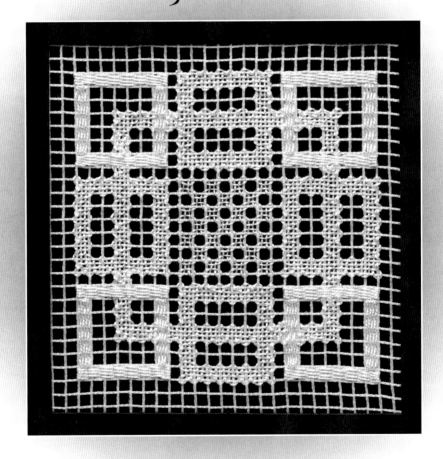

**Worked on 9 count net, using DMC Pearl 12 for
darning stitch and linen stitch and sewing cotton
for oblique loop stitch.
See stitching instructions on page 50.**

HOLES: EXCEPTIONS TO THE RULE

Working holes in parallel lines

When holes are in parallel lines the normal rule for
working holes must be broken, for otherwise a section of
the design will be left unworked (see diagram 13a). In
this lesson you will work a small square of linen stitch
with a central row of linen stitch which divides the
square and means that the holes either side of this row
are parallel to each other. Parallel rows of holes can be
wider apart than this, and sometimes you may not
notice that there are parallel rows of holes until you
work the design and discover that part of the design is
missing a thread. If this happens you can work the
missing thread in afterwards.

To work the holes you make a 360° turn at each hole
in the centre row except the last hole, where you turn
and edge stitch along the loops back to the outer section
of the square (see diagram 13b). Then you complete the
square following the normal rules for linen stitch
(diagram 13c).

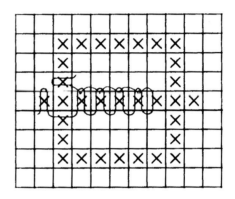

Diagram 13a
Unworked section in
centre of the design

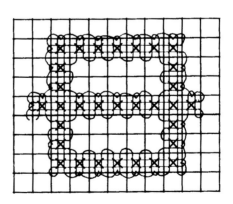

Diagram 13b
Working the centre
section between the
parallel rows of holes

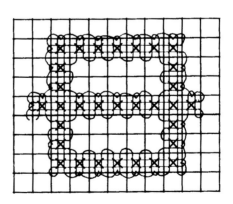

Diagram 13c
The completed design

OBLIQUE LOOP STITCH

Oblique loop stitch, despite its name, is essentially linen stitch worked diagonally, a method that results in every other mesh of the net being left vacant. Consequently it is a more transparent filling than linen stitch or loop stitch, especially when worked with a fine thread.

In oblique loop stitch the first half of each stitch is formed by the upward journey (diagram 14a) and the stitches are completed on the downward journey (diagram 14b and 14c). Because of this, on the upward journey when you weave in each horizontal thread you will encounter a single vertical thread in each square of the net, and you need to allow for the missing thread, which will be added in on the downward journey (i.e. assuming you start with an under, when you put in the horizontal thread you will weave under the bar of the net, over the vertical thread and then over the next bar of the net: under, over, over).

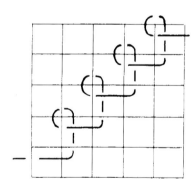

Diagram 14a
Upward journey

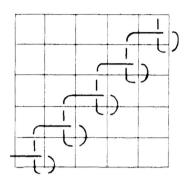

Diagram 14b
Downward journey

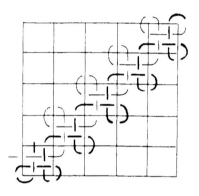

Diagram 14c
Both together: upward
journey light, downward
journey dark

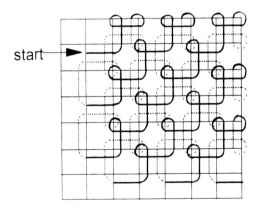

start →

Diagram 14d
Working a square of
oblique loop stitch

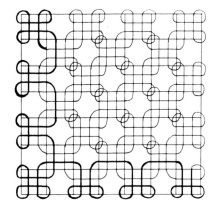

Diagram 14e
Completing the square

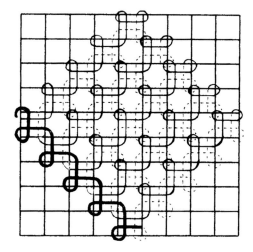

Diagram 14f
Filling a diamond shape

Begin at the spot indicated in diagram 14d, leaving a 10 cm (4 inch) tail. The upward journeys are indicated by the solid black line. The downward journeys are indicated by the broken line. You will note that on each upward journey the thread will loop around intersections of the net which have already been looped around during the previous downward journey (i.e. some intersections end up with two loops of thread around them). By starting at the suggested point, you will end up with a number of half-completed stitches at the bottom and left-hand side of the square. These are worked last and bring the thread back to the starting point, where the beginning and ending threads can be knotted together (see diagram 14e, where the final stitches are shown by a darker line).

Stitching instructions

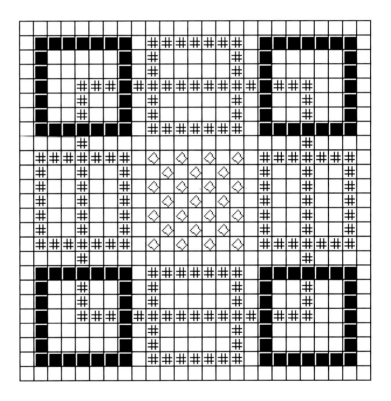

23 meshes wide x 23 meshes high

■ darning stitch

linen stitch

◇ oblique loop stitch

Work the linen stitch sections of the pattern first. In this design the inner sections of the linen stitch squares should be treated as rows of parallel holes (see diagram 13b). Once you have completed the linen stitch, work the darning stitch. Finally, work the oblique loop stitch.

PRACTICE CHART

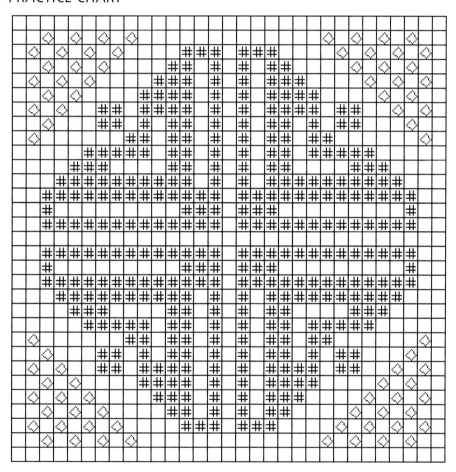

Practice chart for holes in parallel rows and oblique loop stitch

27 meshes wide x 27 meshes high

\#   linen stitch

◇   oblique loop stitch

In this pattern the oblique loop stitch is in the shape of a triangle rather than a square, which is actually simpler to work than a square. Work the triangle at the bottom right of the chart first, starting at the left-hand side (as in diagram 14a). Leave the bottom line of stitches half-completed (as in diagram 14d), until you stitch the final row and end up back where you started. To work the other corners, just rotate your hoop and work each corner in the same way as the first.

Lesson 5
Linen stitch and simple wheels

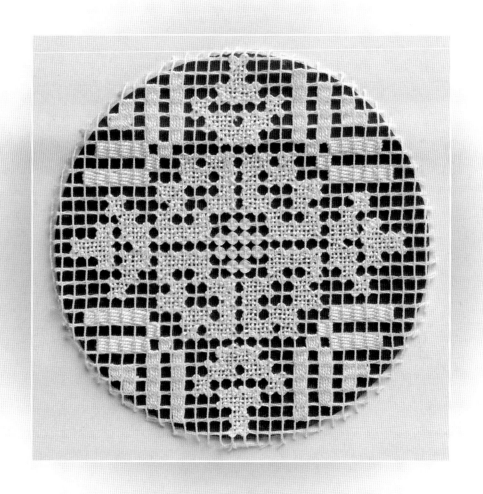

**Worked on 9 count net, using DMC Pearl 12 for
darning stitch and linen stitch, and sewing cotton
for the wheels.**
See stitching instructions on page 55.

WHEELS

These wheels are worked around the intersections of the
net. The wheels can be as small or as large as desired (but
not extending more than halfway across the space
between the threads of the net). Knot your thread at an
intersection of the net—this will be the centre of your
first wheel. Work the wheel by weaving around in a
circle, over and under the net threads, finishing at the
spot nearest to where your next wheel will be. Whip
along the bar of the net to get to the centre of your next
wheel, and complete that wheel in the same way.
Continue in this fashion until all the wheels have been
worked.

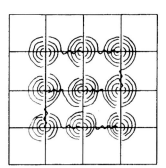

Diagram 15 Wheels

Stitching instructions

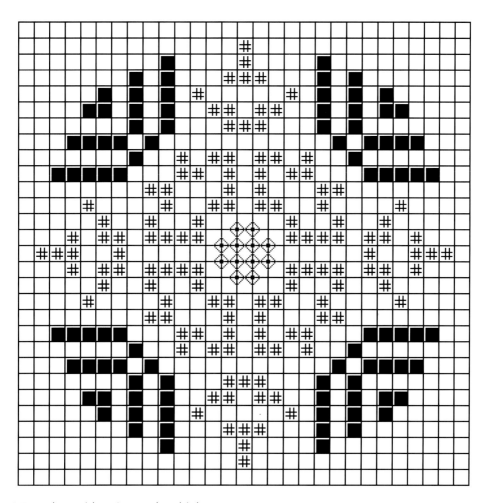

27 meshes wide x 27 meshes high

■   darning stitch

linen stitch

◈   wheel

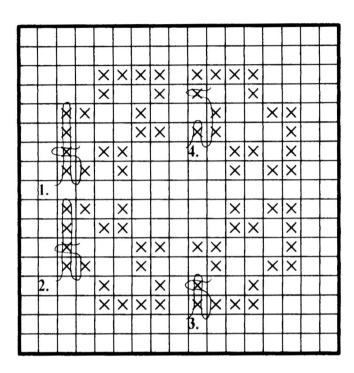

Central section

This central section of the design consists of one shape which is simply rotated 90° to build up a symmetrical design. Treat the vacant area inside the linen stitch shape as a group of holes.

Use this section to practise starting at different points on the chart.

The numbers on the graph above indicate four different suggested starting points. By starting at different points you gain practice in working out your route and also meet with different challenges.

Starting point 1 This is the easiest route and presents no difficulties.

Starting point 2 This is slightly more difficult, as at one point you have to cross a square of the net where you have darned in one thread, but the second thread still remains to be put in. You will have to allow mentally for the missing thread, and make sure that you weave the correct sequence of overs and unders.

Starting point 3 Fairly straightforward, but an example of the fact that you sometimes have to edge stitch into stitches which are incomplete.

Starting point 4 More cases of single threads to contend with.

Filet Lace: Stitches and Patterns

PRACTICE CHART

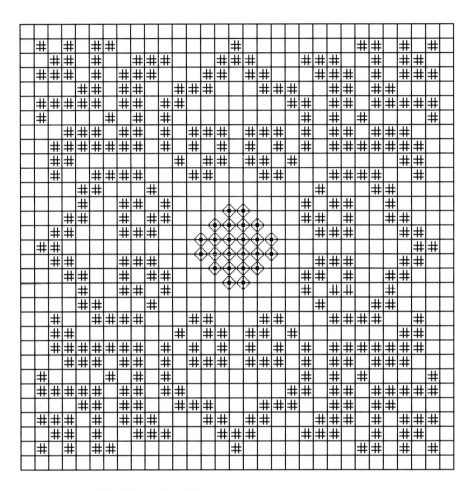

29 meshes wide x 29 meshes high

\#   linen stitch

◇   wheel

Lesson 6
Cross stitch filling, and flower no 1

Worked on 9 count net, using DMC Pearl 12 for linen stitch. and sewing cotton for cross stitch filling and flowers.
See stitching instructions on page 61.

CROSS STITCH FILLING

Following diagrams 16a–16b, knot the thread at the intersection of the net at the top left-hand corner of the square to be worked (you could start at the bottom—just reverse the following instructions). Carry the thread down diagonally over one mesh of the net, under the intersection of the net, and then back up diagonally over one mesh of the net. Continue in this way to the end of the row. Whip down one bar of the net and then repeat the above process in the opposite direction, thus forming a row of crosses. Work the next rows in the same way, until the square is complete.

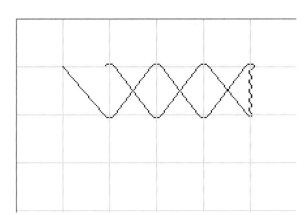

Diagram 16a First row of cross stitch filling

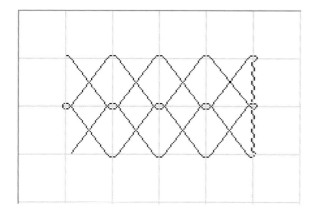

Diagram 16b First two rows of cross stitch filling

Stitching instructions

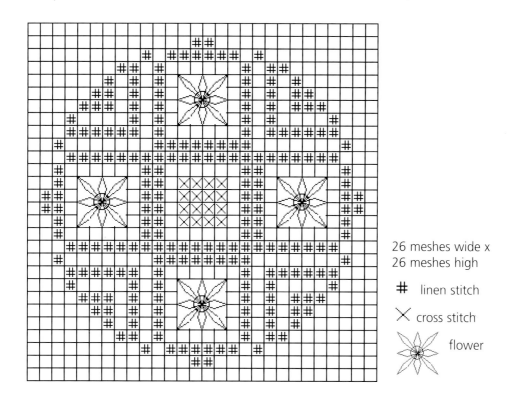

26 meshes wide x
26 meshes high

\#   linen stitch

✕   cross stitch

❋   flower

Work the linen stitch first. Note that the linen stitch has holes which form parallel lines and holes which form a square. Next, work the cross stitch filling in the centre square. Finally, work the flowers.

Flower no 1

Following diagrams 17a–17c, each flower is worked over a square of 4 meshes of the net. Knot your thread at the centre of the square. With your thread in front of the net, carry it diagonally up to one corner, around behind the intersection of the net and then down to the opposite corner of the square. Continue in this way until the required number of threads has been laid down (in the flower for lesson 6 the number was three). Bring the thread back into the centre and change directions in order to work the other diagonal (see diagram 17a).

Bring the thread back into the centre. Now work the vertical threads in the same manner, followed by the horizontal (see diagram 17b).

Bring the thread back toward the centre, but weave under the adjacent group of diagonal threads. Continue weaving in a circle at the centre of the flower, weaving under the diagonal threads and over the horizontal and vertical threads (see diagram 17c). To finish off, take the thread to the back of the work and knot it to an intersection of the net. The finished flower should sit on top of the meshes of the net.

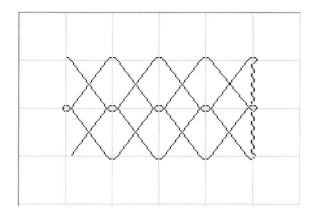

Diagram 16b First two
rows of cross stitch filling

Stitching instructions

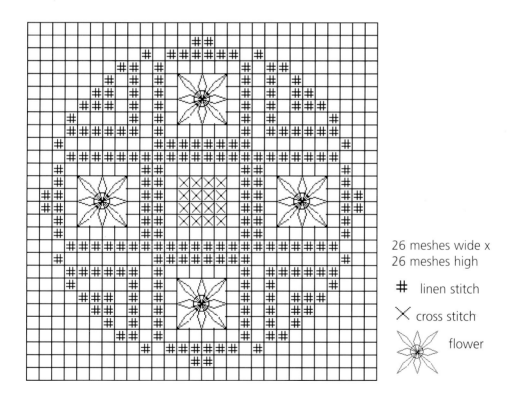

26 meshes wide x
26 meshes high

linen stitch

⨯ cross stitch

    flower

Work the linen stitch first. Note that the linen stitch has holes which form parallel lines and holes which form a square. Next, work the cross stitch filling in the centre square. Finally, work the flowers.

Flower no 1

Following diagrams 17a–17c, each flower is worked over a square of 4 meshes of the net. Knot your thread at the centre of the square. With your thread in front of the net, carry it diagonally up to one corner, around behind the intersection of the net and then down to the opposite corner of the square. Continue in this way until the required number of threads has been laid down (in the flower for lesson 6 the number was three). Bring the thread back into the centre and change directions in order to work the other diagonal (see diagram 17a).

Bring the thread back into the centre. Now work the vertical threads in the same manner, followed by the horizontal (see diagram 17b).

Bring the thread back toward the centre, but weave under the adjacent group of diagonal threads. Continue weaving in a circle at the centre of the flower, weaving under the diagonal threads and over the horizontal and vertical threads (see diagram 17c). To finish off, take the thread to the back of the work and knot it to an intersection of the net. The finished flower should sit on top of the meshes of the net.

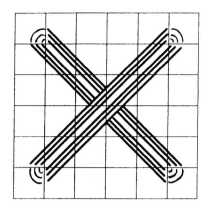

Diagram 17a
Laying down the
diagonal threads

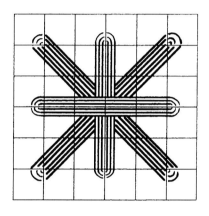

Diagram 17b
Laying down the
horizontal and vertical
threads

Diagram 17c
Weaving the centre of
the flower

PRACTICE CHART

24 meshes wide x 24 meshes high

■   darning stitch

linen stitch

✕   cross stitch

    flower

Lesson 7
Filet Richelieu

Worked on 9 count net, using DMC Pearl 12 for linen stitch and Pearl 8 for the running stitch. See stitching instructions on this page.

The style of filet lace illustrated in this lesson is usually referred to as 'filet Richelieu'. Filet Richelieu is characterised by linen stitch sections outlined and embellished with scrolls and tendrils in running stitch, often worked in a thicker thread.

Stitching instructions

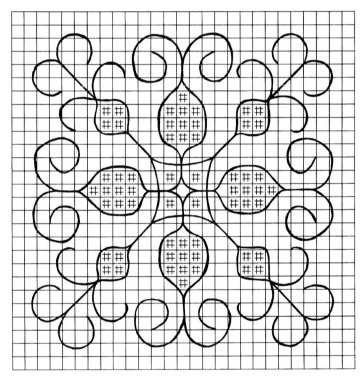

25 meshes wide x 25 meshes high

\#   linen stitch

—   running stitch

Work the linen stitch first, following the chart. Then work the running stitch with a thicker thread.

Running stitch

Starting at the centre of the design, weave the thread over and under the bars of the net to outline the areas of linen stitch and to form the scrolls. When working the scrolls, weave to the centre of the scroll and then go back over the same route, whipping the thread already laid down, to get back to a position where you can work the next scroll or proceed to the next area of linen stitch to be outlined. The scrolls will thus consist of two thicknesses of thread, whereas the outlining thread will be single thickness. In this design, first complete the horizontal and vertical scrolls before starting on the diagonal scrolls. To finish off, knot your beginning and ending threads together and hide the ends at the back of the work.

PRACTICE CHART

39 meshes wide x 39 meshes high

linen stitch

On this chart only the linen stitch is shown. Use the photograph of the finished practice design as a guide for the running stitch.

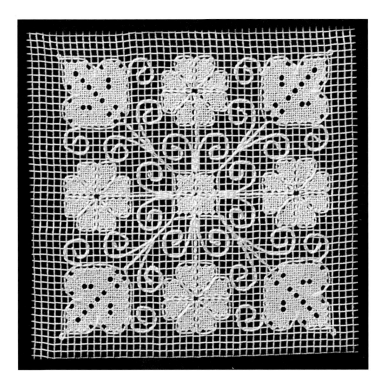

This design is from an old book of patterns called *Le Filet Richelieu*, by Therese de Dillmont (no date, plate no. 30). This book has been reprinted by Lacis Publications in a book entitled *Filet Lace: Techniques for Embroidery on Net*. For those wishing to try the Richelieu style of filet lace, this publication is well worth obtaining. See the bibliography at the back of this book for details.

Lesson 8
Guipure stitch and diagonal stitch

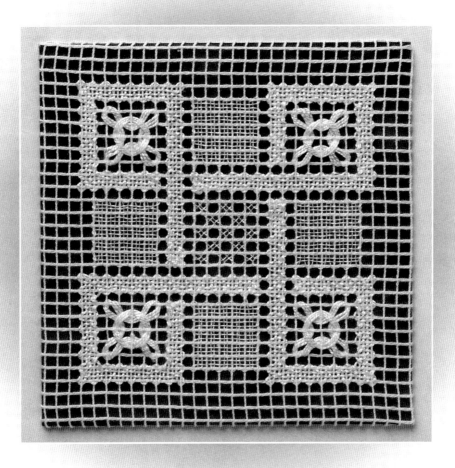

Worked on 9 count net, using DMC Pearl 12 for the linen stitch Celtic-knot border, and sewing cotton for the linen stitch blocks, diagonal filling stitch and guipure stitch.
See page 75 for stitching instructions.

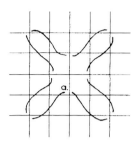

Diagram 18a
Guipure stitch, step 1

GUIPURE STITCH

This stitch is a raised stitch which does not appear to have a specific name; for want of a better term I call it guipure stitch.

Following diagrams 18a–18b, darn the outer path first (step 1). Leaving a tail at the back of your work, and starting at point a, go around the path three times, finishing at the starting point. Take your thread to point b and begin darning the inner path (step 2), taking your thread over the top of the outer threads. Darn around this path two or three times (this depends on the net and thread that you are using), ending back at your starting point. Knot the beginning and ending threads together at the back of the work and hide the ends.

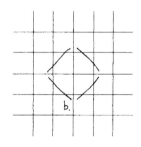

Diagram 18b
Guipure stitch, step 2

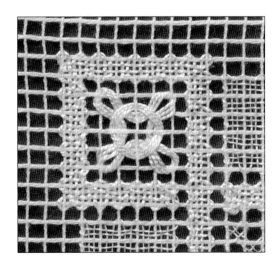

DIAGONAL FILLING STITCH

With diagonal filling stitch, illustrated in diagrams 19a–19f, every other mesh of the net is filled with stitching, which gives a very delicate effect.

To fill a square shape

There are two ways to work a square of diagonal stitch: either by using a single thread and where necessary whipping to the next row to be worked (diagrams 19a–19c), or by using two threads and two different starting points (diagram 19d).

Diagonal filling stitch is worked by weaving your thread diagonally from one side of the square to the other, going around the intersection of the net, and then coming back on the other side of the diagonal row of intersections of the net (this is referred to as row 1). When working a square, your first row up and back will be in one direction, your second row up and back in a different direction (see diagrams 19a and 19b). To begin row 3, loop your thread around the bar of the net and then weave across the square in the same direction as row 1.

To fill a diamond shape

When filling a diamond shape you work all the rows in one direction first, and then work the rows in the other direction (see diagram 19e).

> **HINT** When working all the rows that go in one direction your thread will always go over the *horizontal* bars of the net, and when working the rows that go in the other direction your threads will go over the *vertical* bars (see diagram 19f).

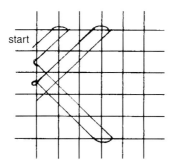

Diagram 19a
Rows 1–3

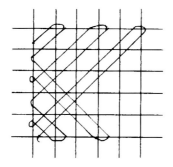

Diagram 19b
Rows 1–5

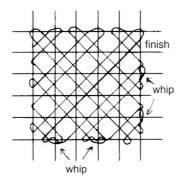

Diagram 19c
Complete the square by
whipping to the start of
the next row

Filet Lace: Stitches and Patterns

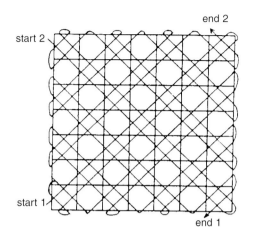

Diagram 19d
Working a square using
two different starting
points

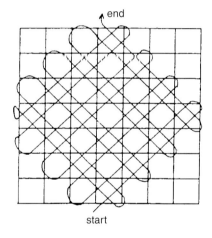

Diagram 19e
Working a diamond
shape

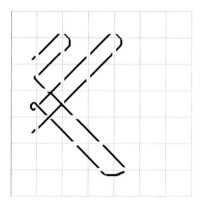

Diagram 19f
Showing how the threads
go over and under the
bars of the net

74

Stitching instructions

23 meshes high x 23 meshes wide

⊞ linen stitch, thicker thread

⌐⌐ linen stitch, finer thread

✖ diagonal stitch

  guipure stitch

Work the four parts of the Celtic knot border in linen stitch. Then work the linen stitch squares using a finer thread. Work the diagonal filling stitch with a fine thread, using the method shown in either diagram 19c or 19d to complete the square. In the vacant spaces in each corner work the guipure stitch, again with a fine thread. When working this stitch, weave around both the outer and inner paths three times.

This design shows how you can use the same stitch with two different weight threads to achieve different textures. You can also use different stitches in conjunction with different weight threads to create perspective. For example, in the simple design shown on page 78 of three trees, the tree in the front is worked in darning stitch, which is a heavy stitch, with Pearl 8. The second tree is worked with Pearl 12 in linen stitch, which is a lighter stitch than darning stitch. The tree in the background is worked with sewing cotton in loop stitch, which is a transparent stitch and gives the effect of the tree fading into the background.

PRACTICE CHART

29 meshes wide x 29 meshes wide

linen stitch

※ diagonal stitch

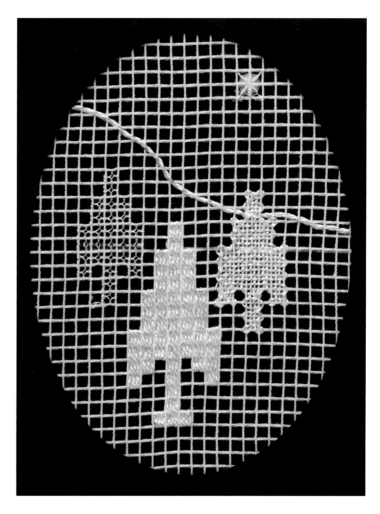

Achieving the effect of perspective with different stitches and thread weights

Lesson 9
Leaves

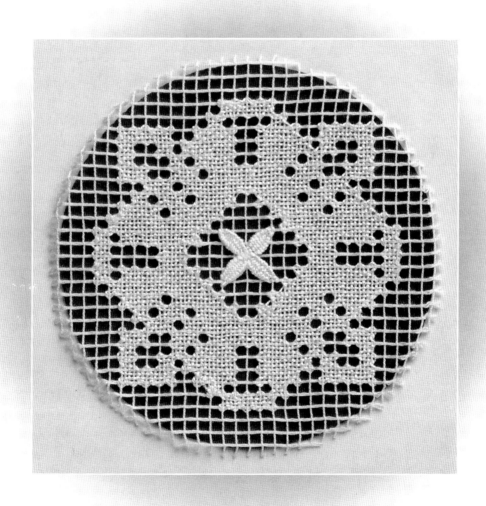

**Worked on 9 count net, using DMC Pearl 12 for
linen stitch and leaves.
See stitching instructions on pages 83 to 85.**

LEAVES

Leaves can be worked with either one central vein or
with two or more veins, and can lie horizontally,
vertically or on the diagonal. They can also be worked on
the net itself or onto a background of linen stitch.

*Leaves with one vein
worked over linen stitch*

*Leaves with two veins
worked straight onto net*

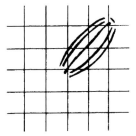

Diagram 20
Laying down the
foundation threads for a
leaf with two veins

Following diagram 20, knot your thread at an
intersection of the net (make sure the knot is at the
back). Bring the thread to the front of the net and take it
diagonally over two holes, behind the intersection of the
net, and back to the starting point. Do this again, and
then take the thread back out to the top of the leaf. You
now have five threads which constitute the foundation
threads for a leaf, two threads for each side of the leaf
and one thread for the centre (diagram 20). Now begin
weaving the leaf, starting at the tip and working towards
the bottom, weaving over and under the foundation
threads (treat the two threads at either side of the leaf as
a single thread, so that you are weaving over a total of
three foundation threads). Pull your weaving tightly at
the tips of the leaf, looser at the centre of the leaf, and
then tight again at the base of the leaf, so that you get a
nice shape.

To work more leaves, as shown in the photograph of
lesson 9, lay down the foundation threads for a second
leaf opposite the first one, and weave that one in the
same way. Repeat for the third and fourth leaves. Take
your thread to the back and secure it. The finished leaves
should lie on top of the net.

It is not always easy to get your leaves looking even
but with practice you can get a good result.

Two long leaves

Another (easier) alternative to working four separate leaves would be to work just two longer leaves, with one lying on top of the other (as in the picture above). Make sure that you weave more tightly at the centre of each long leaf, so as to give the impression that there are four leaves.

Leaf with one vein

These are worked in the same way except that you simply weave over and under the foundation threads at each side of the leaf, that is, you do not have a central thread to weave over.

Stitching instructions

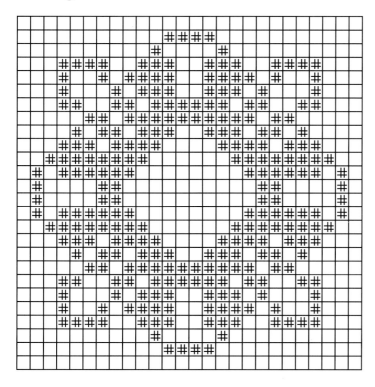

24 meshes wide x
24 meshes high

linen stitch

In this design there are holes which form squares, which makes the linen stitch more complicated. When you attempt a design which you think may present problems in working out the route of the linen stitch, it is a good idea to draw the design on graph paper first (or alternatively photocopy the original, enlarging it if necessary), and then plot out the course of the thread in pencil. If you do this, keeping to the normal rule for holes, it will be obvious when you get back to the starting point whether any sections have not been worked. You can then see where it is necessary to break the normal rule for holes so that these sections can be filled.

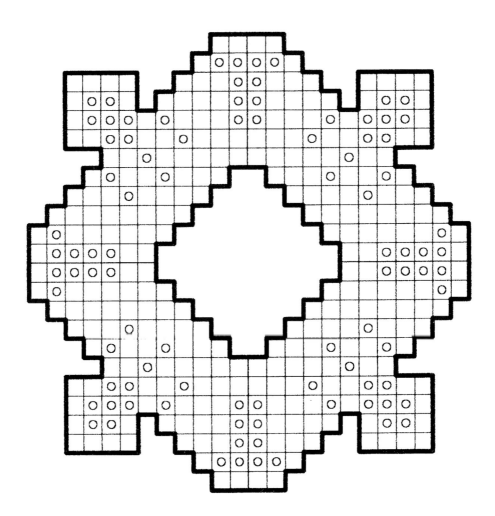

24 meshes wide x
24 meshes high

This graph shows the area to be filled with linen stitch (the blank squares within the heavy outlines). The holes are indicated by a circle. It is suggested that the centre section not be treated as a series of holes. Rather, the inside edge can be made 'loopy' to match the outside edge by working edge stitch all around the inside after the linen stitch has been completed.

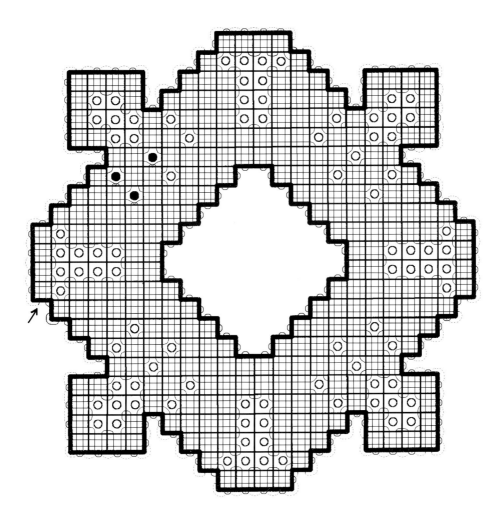

On this graph, a possible route is mapped out for you, starting at the point indicated on the left-hand side. Of course, you could start at a different point, and you may like to practise different starting points on graph paper.

Again, the open circles indicate holes where the normal rule for working holes was followed. The solid circles indicate the holes where the normal rule for holes was broken in order to get to the inside of the square. The dotted lines indicate edge stitch. The inside of the design could also be edge-stitched to make it 'loopy'.

PRACTICE CHART

This pattern is from the sixteenth century pattern book by Federico Vinciolo. For other patterns from this book you can purchase the facsimile edition printed by Dover Publications (see bibliography).

43 meshes wide x 43 meshes high

linen stitch

This pattern in linen stitch has two separate parts: the outer section of the design and the inner section. The latter is the more difficult to work.

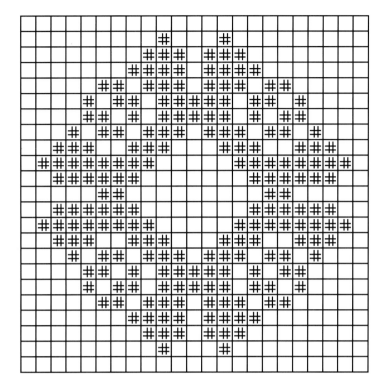

21 meshes wide x
21 meshes high

*Outer part of inner
section*

You can make the inner section easier by dividing it
again into two sections (see charts above and right).
Work the larger outer part first, then the inner. Finally
work edge stitch around the inside edge of the outer
section, so that the holes appear round. This will mean
that two threads will cross where the two sections meet,
making a slightly thicker edge and slightly less distinct
holes.

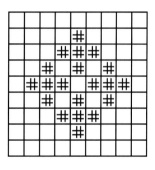

7 meshes wide x
7 meshes high

*Central part of inner
section*

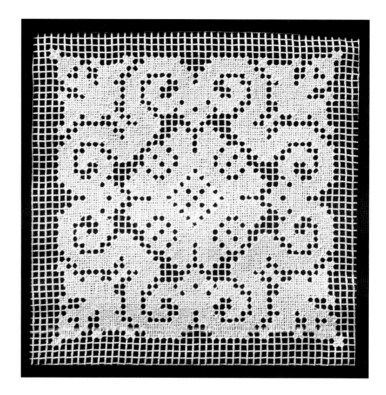

HINT Practise plotting your course on paper first before beginning to stitch. This will show you where the difficulties of the design lie, and where you will need to break the normal rule for holes in order to get to areas which would otherwise be left unworked.

Lesson 10
Cushion stitch, wheels, and outlining stitch

Worked on 9 count net, using DMC Pearl 12 for linen stitch, cushion stitch and outlining stitch, and sewing cotton for oblique loop stitch and wheels.

See chart on page 96.

CUSHION STITCH

Following diagrams 21a–21b, lay threads around the bars of the net for the whole length of the row (do not weave under and over the bars of the net). Do not pull the threads too tight. The more times you wind the threads around the row the more cushioned an effect you will get. See diagram 21a. Now take your thread to the side of the row and begin weaving as shown in diagram 21b. Do not weave over and under each individual thread, but treat the threads you have laid down as a whole unit. The number of times you weave back and forth is a matter of individual choice, but in the photograph below three threads show on the top of the work.

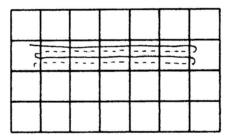

Diagram 21a Laying down the padding threads

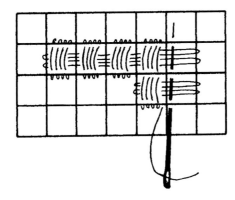

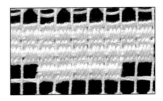

Cushion stitch

Diagram 21b Weaving

WHEELS

Wheels are worked over a square of four meshes of the net. Tie your thread loosely to the net a short distance from where you wish to start the wheel, leaving a long enough tail so that the beginning thread can be sewn in and hidden after the wheel is completed.

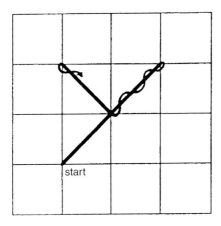

Diagram 22a Carry the thread to the opposite corner of the square. Whip back to the centre. The whipped thread should have the appearance of a cord. Carry the thread out to the next corner. Whip back to the centre.

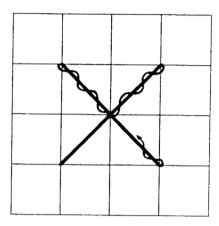

Diagram 22b Carry the thread out to the next corner. Whip back to the centre. You are now ready to work the central spiral. Note that one of the spokes of the wheel is only a single thread at this stage (i.e. it has not been whipped).

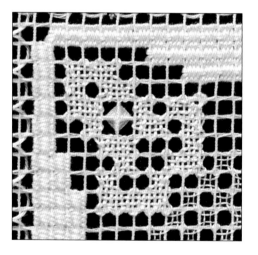

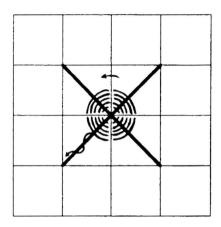

Diagram 22c Darned wheel: Darn over and under the threads of the net and the diagonal whipped threads until the wheel is the desired size. To finish off, either stop opposite the single spoke, darn through the back, and then whip out to the corner along the single thread, or finish the wheel next to the single thread and whip out tightly (it needs to be tight in order to keep the wheel a good shape) to the outside corner.

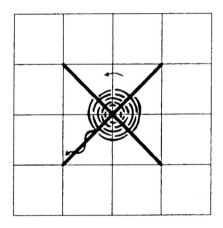

Diagram 22d Woven wheel: In needle lace a woven wheel (sometimes called a spider) has an uneven number of spokes or legs. In filet lace the number is even (8), and therefore it is necessary to cheat a little to get the same result. Proceed as for the darned wheel, except that at some point in each round of the spiral you need to go under two adjacent spokes so that you get a woven effect.

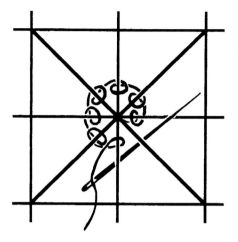

Diagram 22e Ribbed wheel: Work the spokes as above. To make the wheel work a back stitch over one spoke, and then pass the needle under two spokes. Continue in this way (over one, under two), until it is the desired size. The result will be a rib along each spoke. Finish off as above.

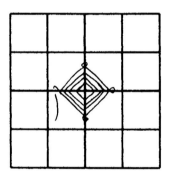

Diagram 22f Woven diamond: This is similar to the ribbed wheel, except that diagonal threads are not laid down first. Thus there are only four threads to weave around and the resulting shape is a diamond rather than a circle. The diamond can be worked with the ribs at the front or at the back. Knot the thread to the centre of the square and weave around the four threads until the desired size is reached. To finish off, whip out along the bar of the net and knot the thread to an intersection of the net.

OUTLINING STITCH

Outlining stitch is a very simple stitch. It is worked in two journeys. Firstly weave over and under the net as shown in diagram 23a, and then come back working the second half of the stitch, as shown in diagram 23b.

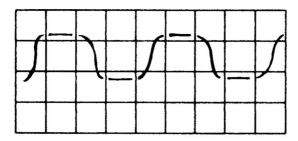

Diagram 23a First half of outlining stitch

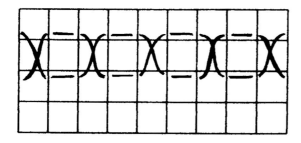

Diagram 23b Second half of outlining stitch

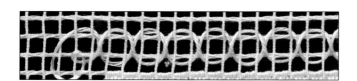

Stitching instructions

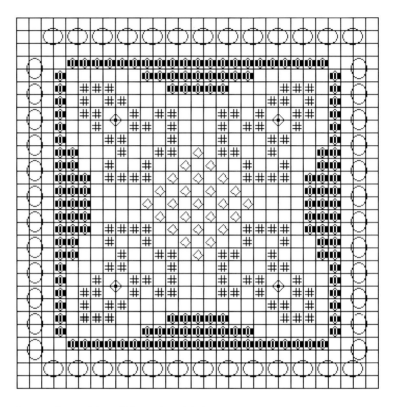

27 meshes wide x 27 meshes high

▥ cushion stitch

\# linen stitch

◇ oblique loop stitch

◈ wheel

○ outlining stitch

Work the linen stitch sections first, and then work the other stitches.

PRACTICE CHART

40 meshes wide x 40 meshes high

linen stitch

◈ wheel

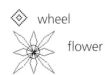 flower

For this chart you can choose which filling stitches you work in the vacant areas. The stitches used in the pictured example are oblique loop stitch, diagonal filling stitch, wave stitch, and diamond filling stitch (see diagrams 14, 19, 25 and 26 for these stitches). Leaves (see diagram 20) were also worked in the centre square.

Samplers and extra stitches

SAMPLER 1

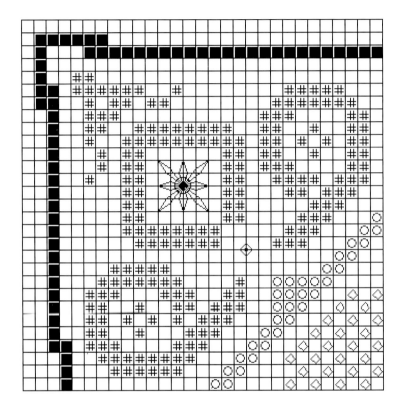

56 meshes wide x 56 meshes high;
note only one quarter of design graphed

■ darning stitch

linen stitch

○ loop stitch (optional)

◇ oblique loop stitch (optional)

◈ wheel (optional)

✳ flower (optional)

The graph shows one quarter of the sampler pattern design. This design is included so that you can experiment with various stitches. (You do not need to use the same stitches as those illustrated.)

Work the linen stitch first, and then decide which filling and raised stitches you wish to use.

SAMPLER 2

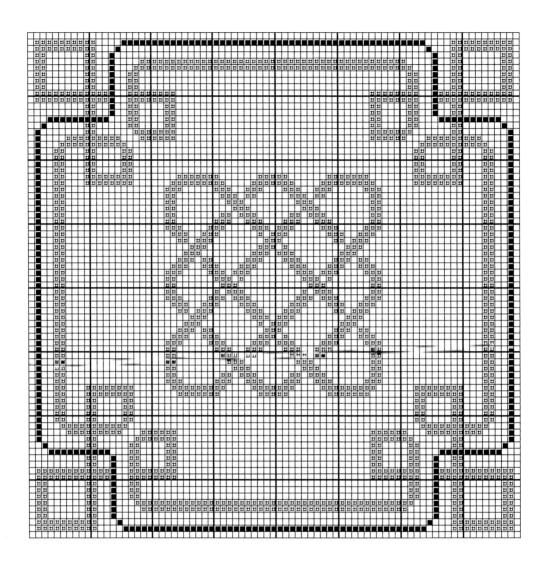

77 meshes wide x 77 meshes high

■ darning stitch

\# linen stitch

Stitch the linen stitch and darning stitch as shown on the chart, and then choose filling stitches and raised stitches to place in the vacant spaces.

FLOWER NO 2

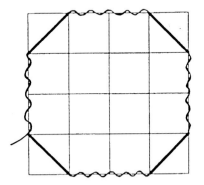

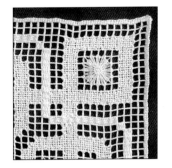

Diagram 24a Whip along the sides of two meshes of the net. Carry the thread diagonally across the next mesh, and then whip along the sides of two more meshes. Carry the thread diagonally across the next mesh. Continue in this fashion until you get back to where you started.

This flower is worked over a square of 4 x 4 meshes of the net

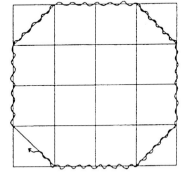

Diagram 24b Whip along the same route again, making sure that the diagonals are firmly whipped.

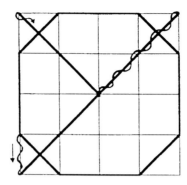

Diagram 24c Whip down to the corner of the square. Carry the thread diagonally across to the opposite corner of the square, weaving it over and under the net threads, and then whip back to the centre. Make sure that the diagonal thread at the corner of the square is anchored in position between the whipped and the whipping threads.
Work out to another corner.

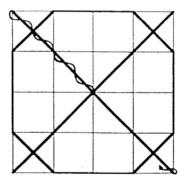

Diagram 24d Whip back to the centre and then weave out to the opposite corner.

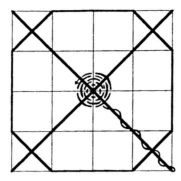

Diagram 24e Whip back to the centre again and then weave a wheel in the centre of the square.

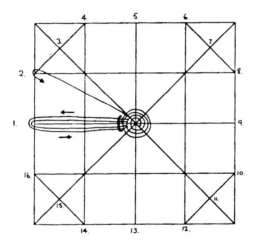

Diagram 24f Carry the thread into the wheel to make the first petal. The wheel is used as a base for the petals by working the thread into the wheel on each turn. Work each petal in an anti-clockwise direction. Carry the thread out from the wheel, over two net threads to the outside edge of the square, turn, and come back into the centre. Repeat once more. Gather the petal threads together at the base and then come up in position ready to work the next petal. Work 16 petals.

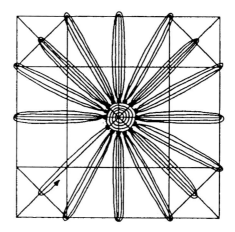

Diagram 24g This diagram shows the almost completed flower. Complete the petals. Secure the thread at the back of the wheel, or whip out in order to work another flower.

WHEELS: VARIATIONS

VARIATION OF GUIPURE STITCH

WAVE STITCH

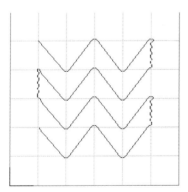

Diagram 25 This simple filling stitch is worked in rows and the height of the stitch can extend over one or more rows of the net

DIAMOND FILLING STITCH

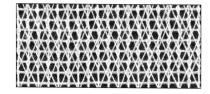

Diamond filling stitch is essentially overlapping rows of herringbone stitch

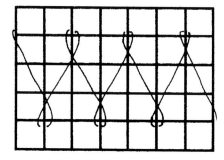

Diagram 26a First row

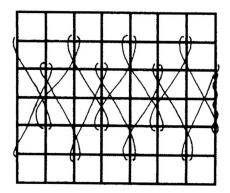

Diagram 26b Second row added

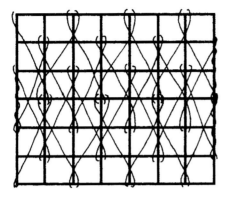

Diagram 26c Third row added

CIRCULAR BORDER STITCH

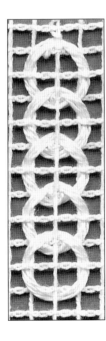
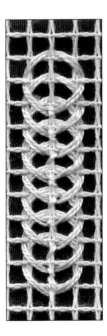

This stitch can be worked horizontally or vertically. It is worked over four meshes of the net and consists of overlapping circles. The number of times you work around each circle depends on the net you are using and the effect you wish to achieve. The circles can be spaced only one square apart from each other so that they overlap, or they can be spaced two squares apart so that they are further apart, touching only at the edges. To get from one circle to the next you simply whip down the net thread in the centre of the circle until you get to the position to start the next circle, or you work an extra half-circle to get to the start of the next circle.

There are other variations to this stitch. One such variation is used in the mat on page 135, where the stitch is worked horizontally, with each stitch extending over three meshes of the net (i.e. over four threads of the net). Begin the border as shown in diagram 27a, and then continue as in diagram 27b (i.e. you go under two horizontal threads in the centre, and under one vertical thread at the top, but under two *vertical* threads at the bottom). At the end of the row finish off as in diagram 27c. The border is finished off by weaving a thread though the centre of the circles.

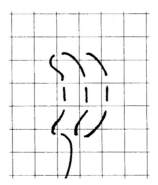

Diagram 27a Beginning circular border stitch

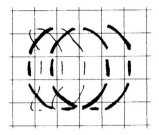

Diagram 27b Working circular border stitch

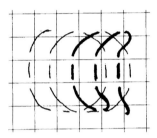

Diagram 27c Finishing circular border stitch

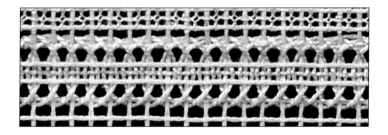

BOW BORDER STITCH

The bow border is another useful border stitch. It can be used as an alternative to the circular border in the pattern for the large Hardanger-inspired mat in Part II: Patterns.

This border is a series of herringbone stitches with loops added. It is worked over four meshes (i.e. five threads). Work the first row of stitches as shown in diagram 28a. Turn your work upside down and work a second row of loops in between the loops of the first row (diagram 28b). To turn the corners, make a motif as shown in diagram 28c. One motif is made while working the first row, the other while working the second row. Make the motifs by working the loops first, and then working a wheel around one end and pulling it tight. Finally, whip along the centre thread of the net, pulling the loops into bows.

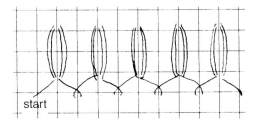

Diagram 28a First row

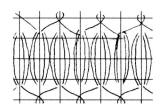

Diagram 28b Second row added

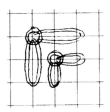

Diagram 28c Corner

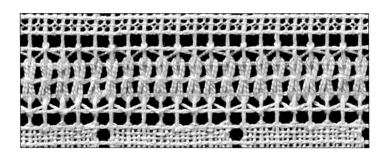

STAR FILLING STITCH

This stitch is worked diagonally and in three parts (although you could stop after the second part, as that still makes a decorative filling stitch). The first part of the stitch is worked in an upwards direction (from bottom left to top right) by taking your needle under the intersection of the net, as in the first picture below. Part two of the stitch is the downward journey, in which you again take your needle under the intersections of the net (see second picture). You repeat this pattern to fill the required area, leaving a gap of one diagonal row of meshes between each row (see third picture). For the final part of the stitch you again work in diagonal rows, taking your thread under the intersections of the net, but this time from right to left, so that the thread crosses over the top of the stitches formed by the previous journeys.

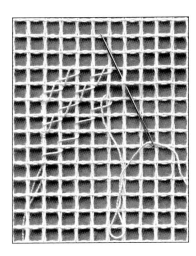

part 1

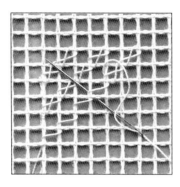

part 2

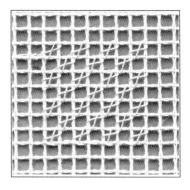

part 2 completed

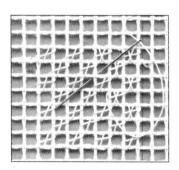

halfway through part 3

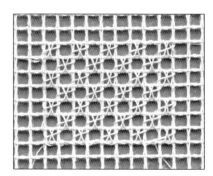

completed stitch

Four styles of filet lace

Clockwise from top left-hand corner: filet guipure, traditional filet, filet Richelieu, Finnish style filet

Detail of Finnish style filet, embroidered on a machine-made net

Finnish style mat: on hand-knotted net and embroidered by the author

Wedding charms

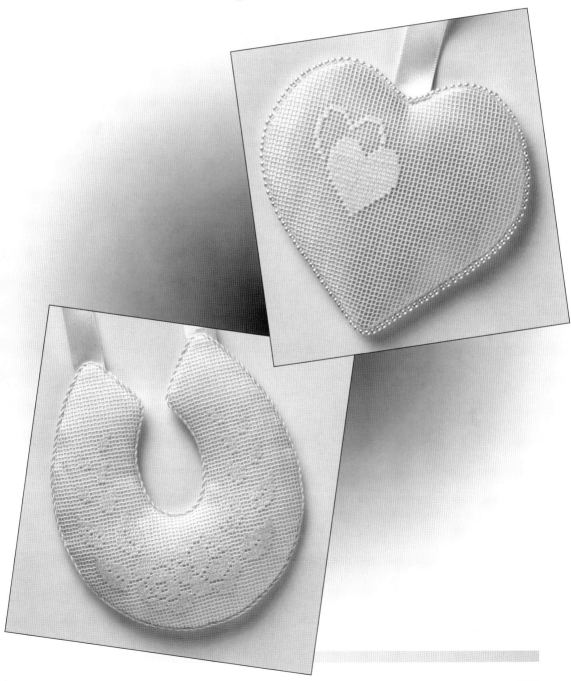

Both these charms were stitched in darning stitch on 14 count net, using DMC Pearl 12.

22 meshes wide x 23 meshes high

■ darning stitch

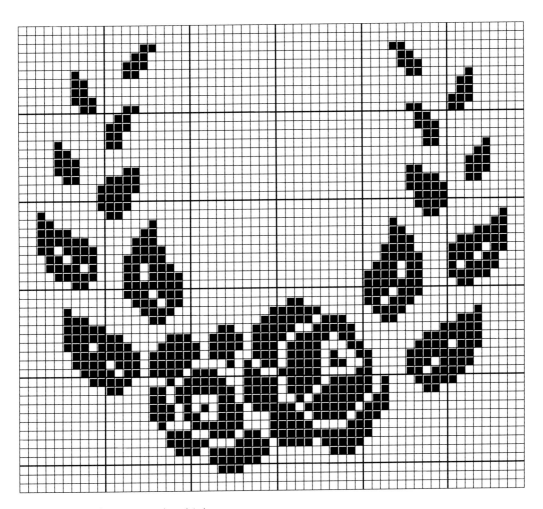

55 meshes wide x 49 meshes high

■ darning stitch

Making up instructions

The instructions for both charms are the same. Using the templates, cut out two cardboard shapes (i.e. a back and a front). Pad both with batting, using a single layer for the back and a double layer for the front. Cover both back and front with white or cream material, using the calico and lace technique, that is, two pieces of cardboard are padded and covered with fabric. Using the same technique, cover the front with the lace. Put the front and back together, with ribbon for the hanging inserted between them, and sew them together. To cover the join, either make a cord and sew it all around the edge, or sew beads around the edge.

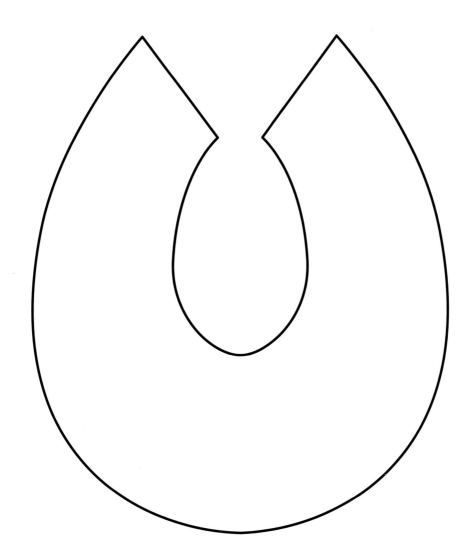

Pot lid and soap bag

**Both these items were stitched in darning stitch
on 14 count net, using DMC Pearl 12.**

Graph for pot lid: 40 meshes wide x 40 meshes high

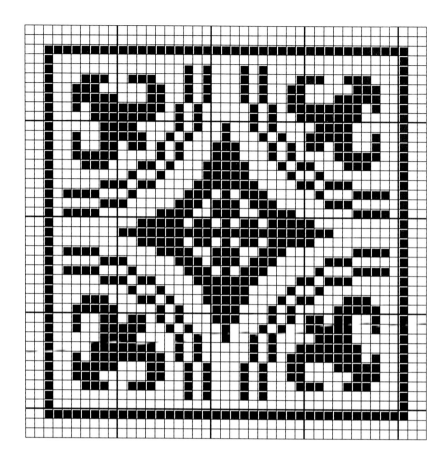

Graph for soap bag: 39 meshes wide x 39 meshes high

This graph could be made into a larger design by treating it as a repeat pattern. If you do this, omit the border and make the repeat patterns touch, so that they fit together like tiles (see tile graph).

Repeat design created from soap bag motif

Tray
A flowing design mounted in a glass-based tray

This design was worked on 9 count net, and the finished lace was mounted in a tray with a glass base (the border of darning stitch was omitted). The lace could also be made into a doily. In this case, work the border and finish off by working a buttonhole stitch edging one row out from the border. The finished size of the doily would be approximately 26 cm (10¼ inches) wide.

94 meshes wide x 94 meshes high

■ darning stitch, DMC Pearl 12, white   # linen stitch, DMC Pearl 12, white

○ loop stitch, DMC Broder Machine 30 or similar thread

Wattle mat

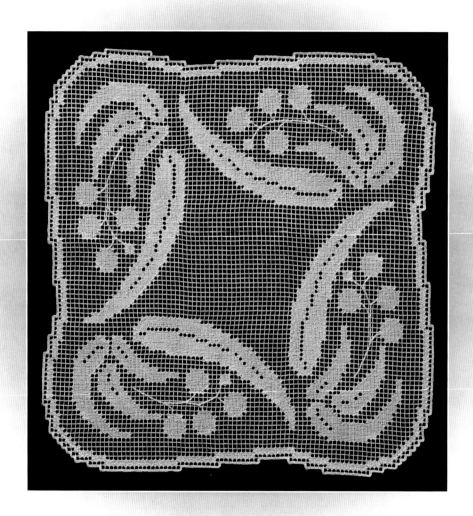

Finished size of the wattle mat approximately 25 cm (10 inches) square

The wattle mat was worked on 9 count net in linen stitch, using DMC Pearl 12.
The stems were worked in whipped running stitch.
It could be worked in darning stitch instead of linen stitch.

89 meshes wide x 89 meshes high

Floral mat

The floral mat was worked on 9 count net; finished size approximately
30 cm (12 inches) square

The graph shows one quarter of the design. By rotating the chart 90°, you can use it to stitch all four of the corner flowers and leaves. The centre of the design is marked by the arrows. Make sure that the centre circle is worked as a whole (i.e. not as four separate quarters).

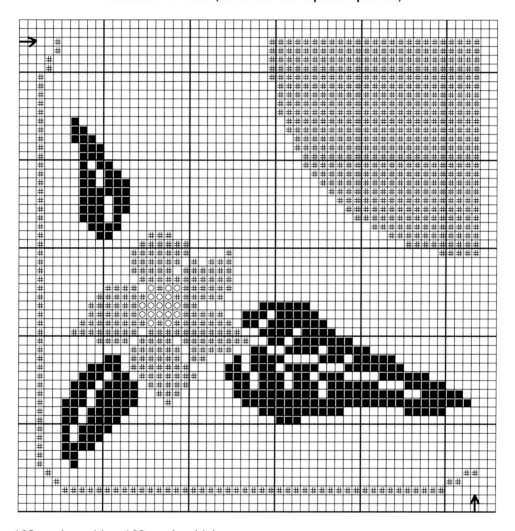

103 meshes wide x 103 meshes high

■ darning stitch, DMC Pearl 12, white

linen stitch, DMC Pearl 12, white

○ loop stitch, DMC Broder Machine 50 or similar thread

Filet mats inspired by Hardanger embroidery

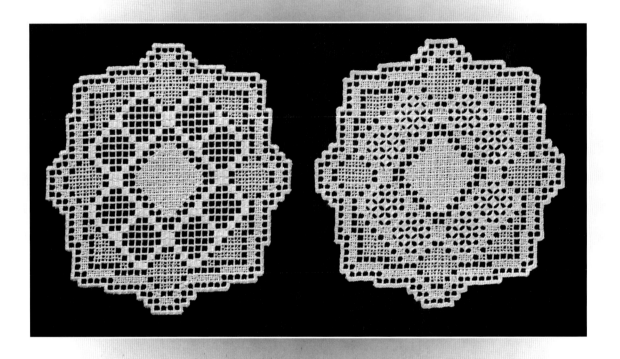

These small mats inspired by Hardanger embroidery were worked on a 6 count net. The buttonhole stitch edging was worked with DMC Pearl 8. Finished size approximately 15 cm (6 inches) square.

TWO SMALL MATS

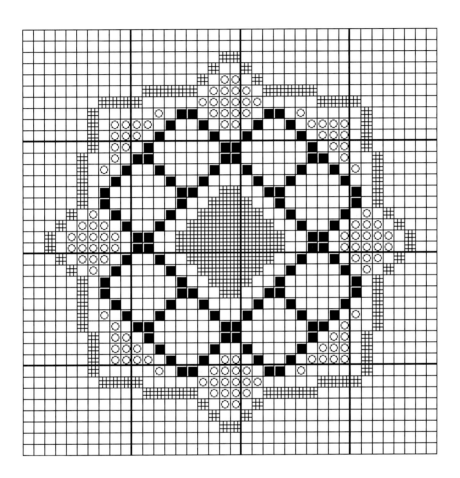

34 meshes wide x 34 meshes high

■ darning stitch, DMC Pearl 8

\# linen stitch, DMC Pearl 8

○ loop stitch, DMC Pearl 12

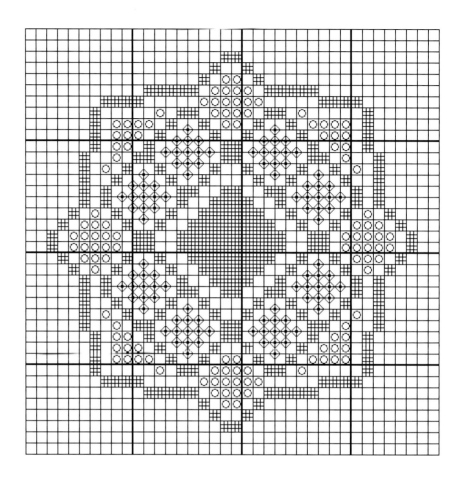

34 meshes wide x 34 meshes high

■ darning stitch, DMC Pearl 8

linen stitch, DMC Pearl 8

○ loop stitch, DMC Pearl 12

◇ wheels, DMC Pearl 12

LARGE MAT

The two versions of the large Hardanger-inspired mat, pictured here and on page 138, each have two rows of 8 blocks of linen stitch (as in the complete graph on page 137). Finished size of both approximately 42 x 21 cm (16½ x 8¼ inches).

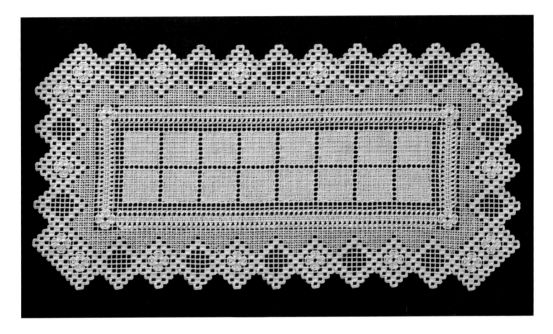

This large Hardanger-inspired mat was also worked on 6 count net.

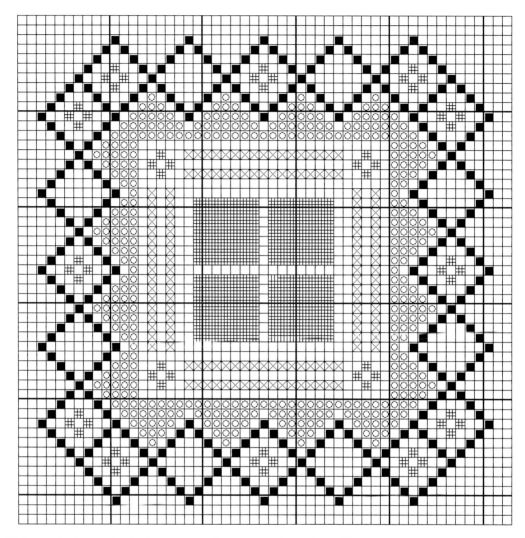

This graph shows the basic pattern. The mat can be enlarged by increasing the number of squares of linen stitch in the centre.

49 meshes wide x 49 meshes high

■   darning stitch, DMC Pearl 8

linen stitch, DMC Pearl 8

○   loop stitch, DMC Pearl 12

        circular inner border DMC Pearl 5 OR bow border, DMC Pearl 8

NOTE The circular border is worked over 4 threads, the bow border over 5 threads. Refer back to diagrams 27 and 28.

The outer buttonhole stitch border, in DMC Pearl 8, is worked one mesh out from the darning stitch.

The four-petalled linen stitch flowers are outlined with DMC Pearl 5 (the flowers can be omitted, as seen in the photograph of the alternative version)

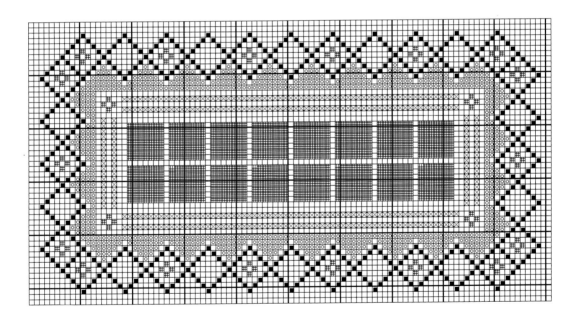

97 meshes wide x 49 meshes high

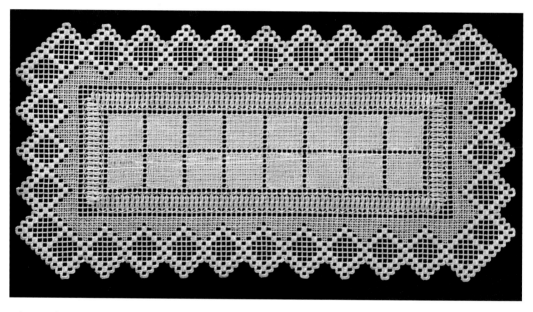

Alternative version of large Hardanger-inspired mat, with the flowers omitted, and circular border replaced by bow border

Variations on an Art Nouveau theme

This small design was worked in darning stitch on 14 count net,
using DMC Pearl 12, and made up into a pincushion

VARIATION 1

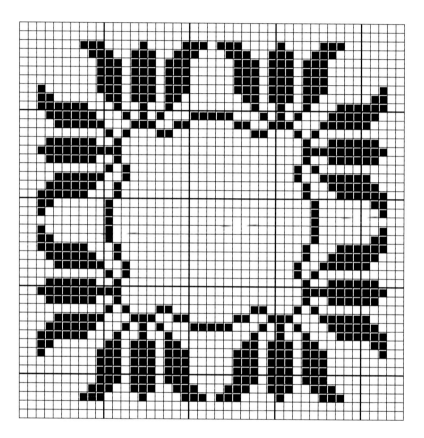

41 meshes wide x 41 meshes high

■ darning stitch

VARIATION 2

This variation was worked on a hand-made net, 10 holes to the inch. However, it could be stitched on a 9 count machine-made net. The embroidery is darning stitch, using DMC Pearl 12.

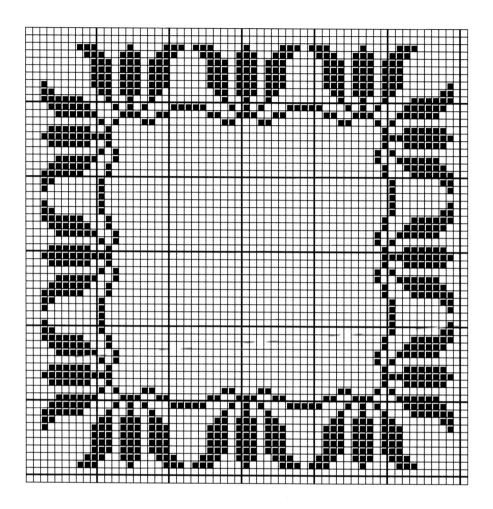

57 meshes wide x 57 meshes high

■ darning stitch

VARIATION 3

For this mat 14 count net was used. For the centre, a piece of linen was hemmed and then slip-stitched on top of the net. The net was not cut away beneath the linen.

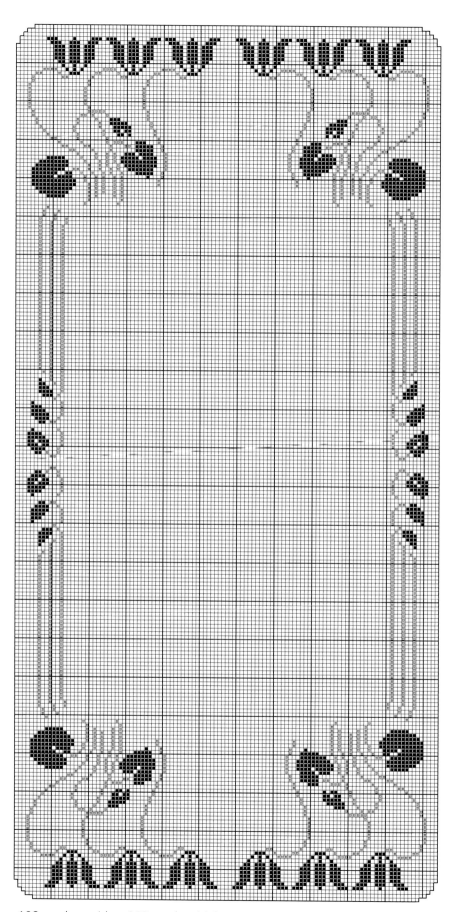

108 meshes wide x 222 meshes high

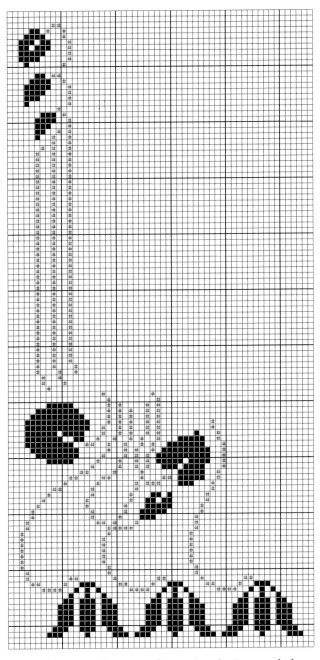

One quarter of the design, enlarged

■ darning stitch, DMC Pearl 12

linen stitch, Brok 36 (this is a thread often used for bobbin lace, but another thread could be used, e.g. DMC Broder Machine 30 or Cordonnet 100).

Buttonhole stitch edge, Brok 36

Leave three meshes out from the design and then stitch the edging. The corners can be rounded off as shown on one end of the reduced graph. Finished size approximately 20 x 40 cm (8 x 16 inches).

Peacock mat

Worked on 14 count net, the finished size of this mat is approximately
36 cm (14 inches) square

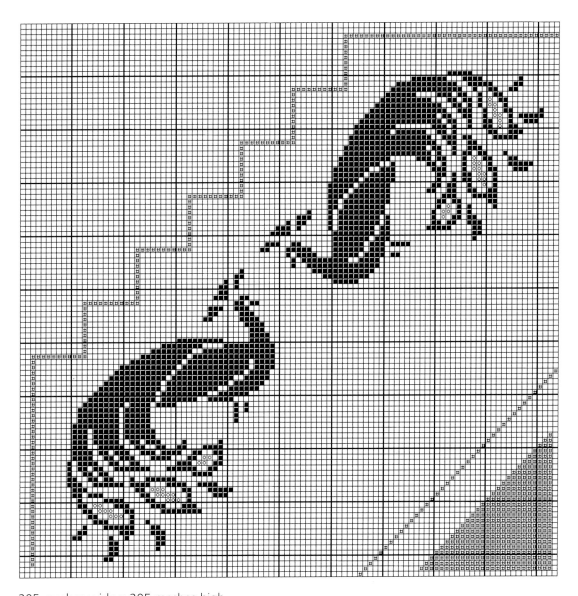

205 meshes wide x 205 meshes high

■ darning stitch, DMC Pearl 12, white

linen stitch, DMC Broder Machine 30, or similar thread

O loop stitch, Kantklosgaren Egyptian cotton 120/2 or similar

Buttonhole stitch edging, DMC Broder Machine 30, or similar

This graph shows one quarter of the design; turn 90° to work each of the other sides of the mat. The complete graph is given in reduced form.

Complete peacock mat graph reduced

Burra

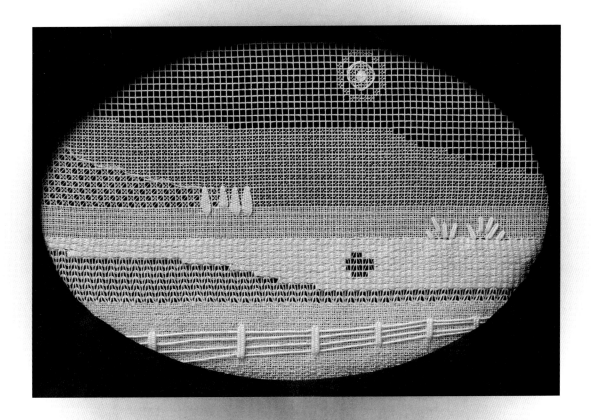

This design was inspired by a photograph of a moonlit lake near the town of Burra in South Australia

Burra was worked on a 9 count net.

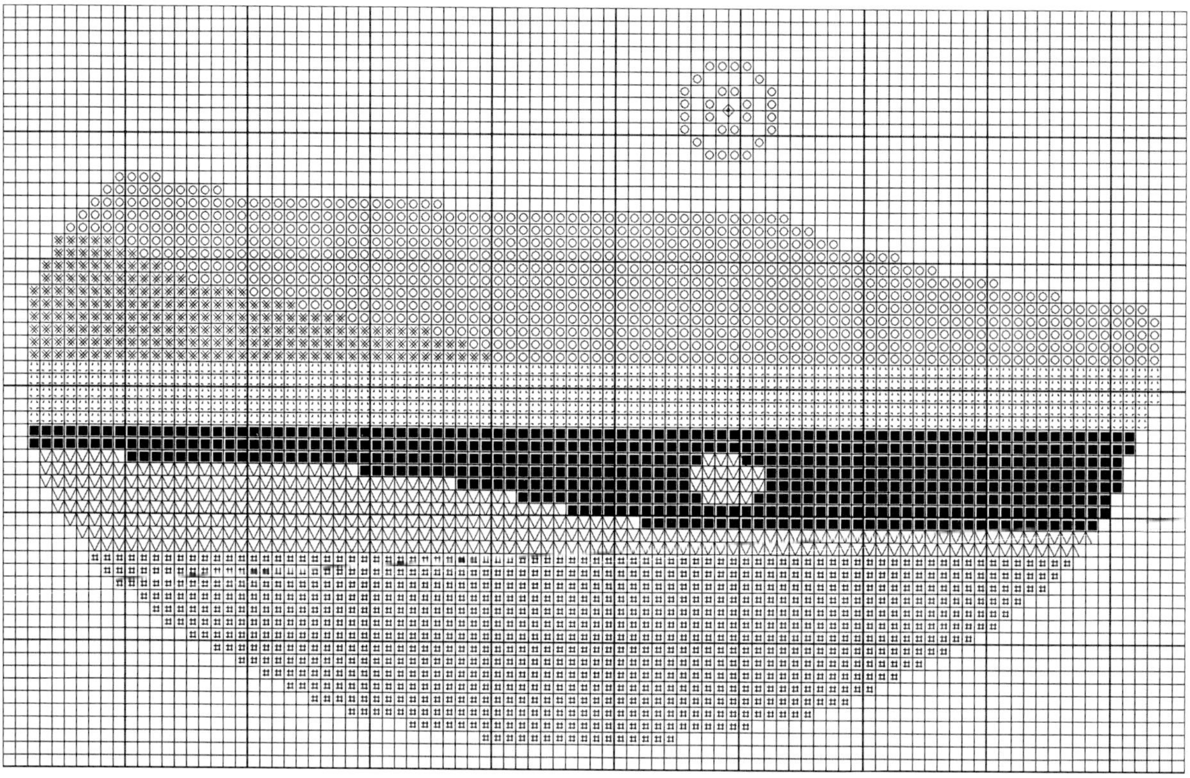

92 meshes wide x 56 meshes high.

Background stitches, from top to bottom:

○ loop stitch, DMC Broder Machine 50

⋇ diagonal stitch, DMC Broder Machine 30

⌟⌞ linen stitch, Brok 60/2 or DMC Broder Machine 30

■ darning stitch, Madeira silk, single strand

.V. wave stitch, DMC Cebelia 20

\# linen stitch 2, DMC Cebelia 40

Raised stitches, from top to bottom:

Moon: ◈ wheel with ◯ loop stitch and running stitch outline, Brok 60/2 or DMC Broder Machine 30

Trees: leaves with three veins (i.e. four foundation threads; see lesson 9), DMC Cebelia 40

Bushes: leaves with one vein (i.e. two foundation threads; see lesson 9), DMC Cebelia 40

Fence posts: leaves with one vein (i.e. two foundation threads; see lesson 9), DMC Cebelia 20

Fence wire (see notes below): DMC Cebelia 10

NOTES

◆ In the diagonal stitch section a single fine thread was run in a diagonal line in the vacant meshes (one direction only), to make this section slightly less open than it would be with diagonal stitch only.

◆ A thicker running thread separates the diagonal stitch area and the loop stitch area above it.

◆ Wave stitch with a fine thread was worked in the small area surrounded by darning stitch.

◆ The fence wires sit on top of the linen stitch and are simply run under the leaves which form the fence post.

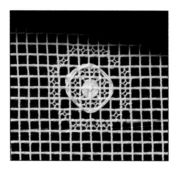

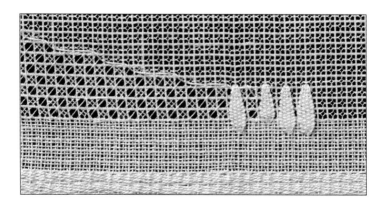

Details of elements of the Burra design

PART III: OLD PATTERNS

The following patterns are taken from early twentieth century filet lace pattern books. They can be worked in either darning stitch or linen stitch.

Square motif 1: cushion insert

Square motifs are useful for mounting in patchwork items

Pattern from Le Filet Ancien, *No. I.*

39 meshes wide x 39 meshes high

Square motif 2

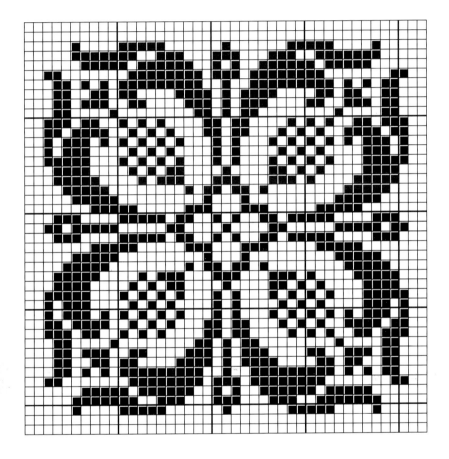

Pattern from Le Filet au Point de Toile, *1st Album.*

39 meshes wide x 39 meshes high

Square motif 3

Pattern from Le Filet Ancien, *No. VII.*

39 meshes wide x 39 meshes high

Square motif 4

Pattern from Le Filet Ancien, *No. I.*

39 meshes wide x 39 meshes high

Elena's mat

Pattern from Le Filet Ancien, *No. III.*

Worked on 9 count net in linen stitch. Finished size approximately
32 by 45 cm (12½ x 17½ inches).

113 meshes wide x 157 meshes high

Curtain trim

Pattern from Le Filet Ancien, *No. VIII.*

Worked on 9 count net in linen stitch. One repeat: 71 meshes wide x 88 meshes high

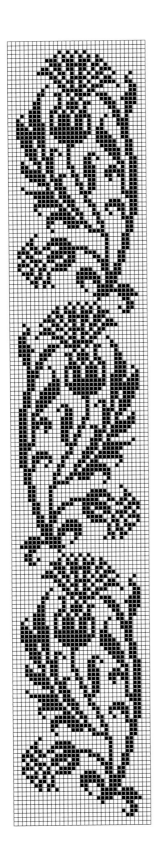

Scotch thistle

Pattern from Le Filet Ancien, *No. V.*

Repeating pattern

One repeat: 62 meshes wide x 29 meshes high

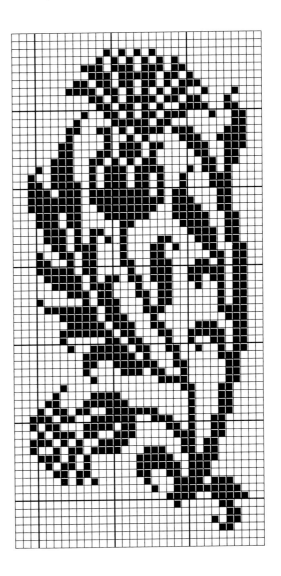

Rose doily

Pattern from Le Filet Ancien, *no. VII.*
197 meshes wide x 197 meshes high

Reticella

Pattern from Le Filet Ancien, *no. VII.*

169 meshes wide x 169 meshes high

Bibliography

Anchor Manual of Needlework, Interweave Press, Loveland, Colorado, 1990

de Dillmont, Therese, *The Complete DMC Encyclopaedia of Needlework*, Running Press, Philadelphia, 1978

Earnshaw, Pat, *Needle-made Laces: Materials, Designs, Techniques*, Collins Australia, Sydney, 1988

Jackson, Mrs F. Nevill, *Old Handmade Lace with a Dictionary of Lace*, Dover Publications, New York, 1987

Kliot, Jules and Kliot, Kaethe (eds), *Filet Lace: Techniques for Embroidery on Net*, Lacis Publications, Berkeley, CA, 2000

Knight, Pauline, *The Technique of Filet Lace*, Batsford, London, 1980

—— *Filet Lace Patterns*, Batsford, London, 1990

Le Filet Ancien au Point de Reprise, Wolf & Dupeyron, Paris, n.d.

Le Filet au Point de Toile, 1st Album, Collection Cartier-Bresson, n.d.

Nouova Enciclopedia dei Lavori Femminili, *Mani di Fata, Milan, 1991*

Swain, Margaret, *The Needlework of Mary Queen of Scots*, Ruth Bean, Carlton Bedford, 1986

Vinciolo, Federico, *Renaissance Patterns for Lace, Embroidery and Needlepoint: an unabridged facsimile of the 'Singuliers et nouveaux pourtraicts' of 1587*, Dover Publications, New York, 1971

Waller, Kathleen, *Introducing Filet Lace*, privately printed, Letchworth, 1987

—— *More Filet Lace*, privately printed, Letchworth, 1990

Stockists

Filet lace nets

Josco Lace Supplies, 101 Ilford Avenue, Arcadia Vale NSW 2283 (mail order)

In the United States the net is available from Lacis, 3163 Adeline Street, Berkeley, CA 94703.

Lacis have also published 11 volumes of *Patterns: Filet Lace*, which are reproductions of many of the pattern books of the early twentieth century.

Stitch index

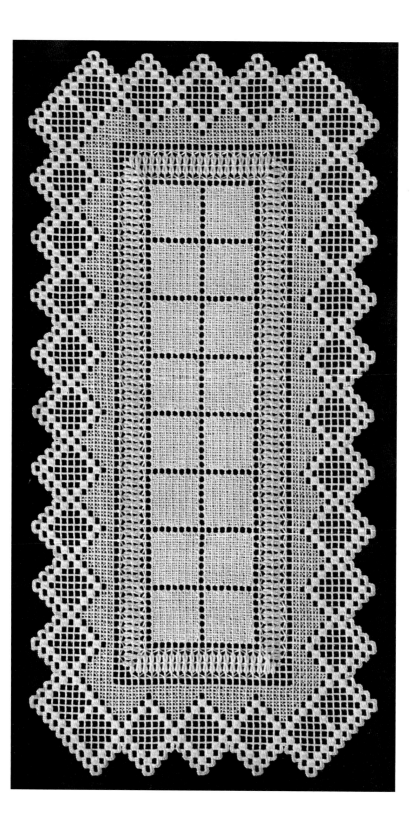